INTEGRATED

COMPUTER PROJECTS

Dr. Lloyd D. Brooks

Department of Management Information Systems
Fogelman College of Business and Economics
The University of Memphis

EMCParadigm
PUBLISHING

Senior Developmental Editor	Sonja M. Brown
Cover and Text Designer	Leslie Anderson
Desktop Production Specialists	Desktop Solutions
Copy Editor	Marjorie Lisovskis
Proofreader	Jean Drury

Publishing Management Team: George Provol, Publisher; Janice Johnson, Director of Product Development; Tony Galvin, Acquisitions Editor, Lori Landwer, Marketing Manager; Shelley Clubb, Electronic Design and Production Manager

Acknowledgments: The author, publisher, and editor wish to thank the following individuals for their valuable insights and suggestions during the development of this text:

Susan Brooks • Information Technology Coordinator, Craigmont High School, Memphis, Tennessee
Michelle Lee • Lead Instructor, Introduction to College Computing, Santa Fe Community College, Gainesville, Florida
Vicki Robertson • Associate Professor, Accountancy, Office Admininstration, and Career Studies Division, Southwest Tennessee Community College, Memphis, Tennessee

Care has been taken to verify the accuracy of information presented in this book. However, the author, editor, and publisher cannot accept any responsibility for Web, e-mail, newsgroup, or chat room subject matter or content, or for consequences from application of the information in this book, and make no warranty, expressed or implied, with respect to its content.

Trademarks: Some of the product names and company names included in this book have been used for identification purposes only and may be trademarks or registered trademarks of their respective manufacturers and sellers. The author, editor, and publisher disclaim any affiliation, association, or connection with, or sponsorship or endorsement by, such owners.

ISBN 0-7638-1899-2

Introduction v

Client 1: International Travel Services   1

Client 2: Athletic House Sports Center   61

Client 3: State Community College Association   121

Introduction

Integrated Computer Projects presents a series of projects for five clients, simulating real-world business activities. Your role will be as coworker and colleague to Ronald Powell, chief consultant for Business Technology Consultants (BTC). BTC provides consulting services for clients requesting projects that require Microsoft® Office applications. The company consists of a professional team of consultants and graphic design specialists who provide information technology solutions to meet the needs of the business community. Typical consulting requests call for the production of one-time documents and include tasks such as providing graphics and a design layout for a brochure, formatting a company newsletter, developing a financial report, and designing a database to be used in a marketing campaign.

Letters, phone calls, and e-mail messages are the primary tools Ronald and his clients use to communicate about projects. Ronald then consults, as needed, with information technology professionals at BTC to obtain additional background for providing the requested services. A full range of word processing, workbook, presentation graphics, database, and multimedia applications are needed for the completion of consulting projects.

Business Technology Consultants has a reputable list of clients who require a high level of expertise for completing a variety of challenging information technology projects. The firm strives to do its best to sustain and enhance the professionalism of each client, with a focus on providing customized care in developing business documents and specialized services that meet the needs of each organization. BTC's goal is to provide clients with top-quality products in an efficient manner and to use effective graphic design and layout techniques that improve the client's image. The corporate motto is: "We provide the best services in the industry. We can do no more. We will not do less."

Your Position

You will become familiar with a variety of activities while working as a consultant for BTC. Yours is an exciting position that demands creativity and originality. A wide range of companies use your consulting services to develop templates, to complete one-of-a-kind documents, and to recommend and develop appropriate design and layout schemes for documents.

Creativity, initiative, and technical skills are required to complete projects in partnership with the chief consultant. Yours is a strategic position, but one that also permits the application of skills in interesting and challenging situations. Although projects are simulated, they are similar to ones that you are likely to encounter in a career that involves using computer and software applications to complete projects in a modern office environment. The jobs comprising each project have been designed to be compatible with office applications software, including Microsoft Office XP.

Skills You Will Use

Projects permit practicing and enhancing many knowledge and skill competencies. You will perform activities such as the following:

- Complete real-world applications relating to the Microsoft Office suite of products.
- Integrate multiple software products while completing projects.
- Demonstrate critical-thinking skills while deciding between alternative approaches.
- Develop independent work habits while also utilizing the team approach to problem solving.
- Select Internet and Web search engine tools for locating information for selected projects.
- Adapt creative approaches to problem-solving activities.
- Utilize multimedia and graphics to enhance document design, layout, functionality, and appearance.
- Analyze real-world business problems and then apply appropriate media and strategy solutions.
- Determine a total problem solution based on an analysis of the components.
- Integrate and reinforce skills and knowledge acquired in previous courses.

Resources Required

You will need to have Internet access to complete certain project activities, specifically to research topics and obtain information that clients have requested. All projects are compatible with Microsoft Office XP, and completing them will require a prior knowledge of Microsoft Office software. Specifically, you should have a working knowledge of and experience with the following software products:

- Microsoft Windows
- Microsoft Word
- Microsoft Excel
- Microsoft PowerPoint
- Microsoft Access

Some projects provide opportunities to work with sound files and animation. One job involves a comprehensive list of multimedia tools including sound, motion, animation, movie, and clip art images. However, sufficient instructions are provided so that prior experience with multimedia tools is not required to complete this particular job.

Design Concepts and Structure

The structure of the applications simulates real-world practices and a realistic work environment. Although projects vary according to the nature of the tasks to be completed, the following scenarios and examples are typical of procedures and job origination processes.

- An e-mail message arrives for Ronald Powell at the offices of Business Technology Consultants. This message normally includes background information needed for the job with comments from the client who sent the message. An example is shown below.

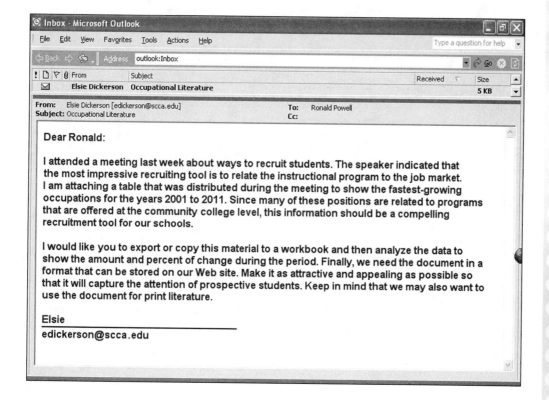

- The e-mail message may include an attachment or refer to a fax that relates to the content of the job. If so, the attachment or fax message will be shown following the e-mail message. For example, the table referred to in the e-mail message above is displayed on the page following the e-mail message, as shown below.

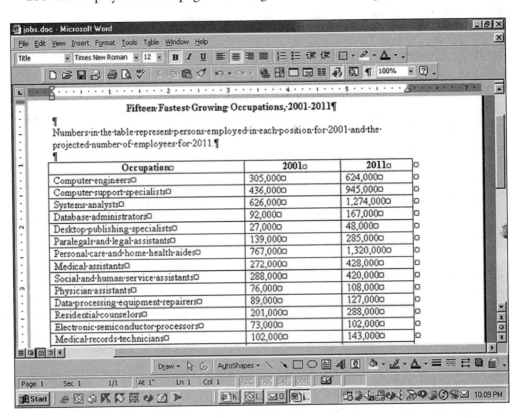

- The file, clip art image, attachment, or other electronically stored media referenced in the e-mail message are included in the student data files created for this book. The files can be downloaded from the Integrated Computer Projects Internet Resource Center, located at the Web site of EMC/Paradigm Publishing. Go to www.emcp.com, click College Division, Internet Resource Centers (under Quick Links at right of window), then click the title *Integrated Computer Projects* under the heading of Computer Applications, and then click Student. Finally, click Student Data Files. The page that displays will provide directions for downloading the files necessary to complete the jobs within each project.

Client Projects

Integrated projects for five clients are included in the program. Large projects require a high degree of structure and standardization in order to be successful. This important management principle was considered when presenting the jobs in this textbook. The work for each client is divided into projects, and each project is made up of one or more jobs. In all, there are 39 projects with a total of 61 jobs to be completed.

While introductory background information about the client is provided with each set of projects, here is a brief description of the five organizations.

 **International Travel Services** 1245 Broadway Terrace • New York, NY 10040	**Client 1:** International Travel Services has franchised agencies in 39 states. The company is a leading provider of electronic global communications with connections to all major airlines, car-rental companies, hotel properties, tour operators, and major cruise lines. This company has been a client for three years. There are five projects (13 jobs) to be completed for this client.
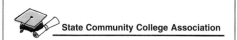 **Athletic House Sports Center**	**Client 2:** Athletic House Sports Center was established in 1986 and has 17 locations in the western United States. The firm uses BTC's services for development of promotional materials, maintaining membership lists, and a variety of other needs. There are seven projects (11 jobs) to be completed for this client.
 **State Community College Association**	**Client 3:** The State Community College Association, with headquarters in Kansas City, Missouri, represents community colleges in the Midwest. BTC provides consulting services relating to student services, faculty and instructional areas, promotional campaigns, financial reports, fund-raising campaigns, and other functions needed by member institutions. There are eight projects (14 jobs) to be completed for this client.
 **RUNYAN MANAGEMENT SERVICES**	**Client 4:** Runyan Management Services is a privately held company that leases and manages office buildings in seven states. The home office is in Boston, Massachusetts. One of the leading property management companies in the industry, the firm depends on BTC to create document layouts, develop forms, and perform other activities that help maintain its corporate image. There are eight projects (12 jobs) to be completed for this client.

Client 5: First South Bank is a diversified financial institution that offers services to regional and national banks as well as over 500,000 retail and consumer customers. The bank depends on BTC for many important activities that require a quick turnaround or expertise relating to Microsoft Office applications. Outsourcing specialized functions is cost-effective and convenient. The bank's home office is located in New Orleans. There are 11 projects (11 jobs) to be completed for this client.

Strategies for Completing Projects

The realistic nature of the projects requires that you review all material relating to each job before beginning to work on the job tasks. These materials include e-mail messages, Job Notes, comments included in the job documents, planning forms provided, and any other information that is available. A "Job Planning" form (shown on the next page) is included with each job (following the job information) to help you organize the tasks and devise a strategy for completing each job efficiently and correctly. Use the Job Planning form to list the documents you need to create, the data files to be downloaded, and the Office programs and features you will use. Unless otherwise directed by your instructor, you should complete this form and attach it to the documents you create for each job. Completing the form gives you advance notice of any software features that seem unfamiliar or complex, so that you can brush up on using the features before you start the job. A similar review of the scenarios before beginning each job provides an overall perspective, or "big picture," about what is included in the job. This perspective will be helpful as you develop a strategy for completing the tasks.

The following Job Planning form has been completed for Client 1, Project 2, Job 1 as an example. You may use this as a model for completing the forms throughout the book. In naming files, consider using the client number, project number, and job number, as in c1p2j1. Place your initials (first, middle, and last name) plus one space before the file name, as in jcb c1p2j1. Check with your instructor about the preferred file-naming scheme. A template for the Job Planning form is available online at the Internet Resource Center, in case you need extra copies of the form.

Job Planning Form

Client: _____International Travel Services_____ Project: ____2____ Job: ____1____

1. What deliverables does the client expect for this job? (Examples include letter, printed report, slide presentation, database file, template, spreadsheet.)

   - PowerPoint slide presentation containing 10–12 slides
   - Web page format document created (or revised) using Word or FrontPage

2. Which additional resources, if any, do you need in finding information to complete the job? (Examples include Internet searches and documents on disk.)

   - Internet: Clip art images
   - Internet: Search engine to locate information on ski resorts
   - Stored files: Workbook file (income.xls) downloaded from Internet Resource Center

3. What software do you need to complete this job?

   PowerPoint, Excel, and Internet Explorer

4. What special software formatting features does the job call for?

   - Link a slide to a workbook file.
   - Create animated bullets.
   - Download graphic images.
   - Apply a slide presentation template.
   - Download appropriate clip art images from a Web site.

STUDENT LOG

Name: ___Jo Bates_____ Date/Time Completed: ___5/17/03, 2 p.m.___

Document File Name(s): _____jcb c1p2j1_____

Comments:
   - The client needs a slide presentation (with clip art) that lists attractions provided at 8 to 10 ski resorts. A presentation template must be applied to all slides.
   - The list of ski resorts is provided on a Web page.
   - One slide for each resort plus title and closing slides is needed.
   - One slide must link to a workbook file. Animated bullets are required.

Internet Searches

A review of using the Internet to locate information is available as an appendix at the end of the textbook. This section provides a list of popular search engines, some tips for using search engines to locate the information you need, some practice activities, and a list of helpful Web sites.

Student Data Files

As noted in the section about strategies for completing the projects, certain jobs include data files that have been prepared for you. The file names are listed in the Job Notes section for each job, and you should download the appropriate file folder from the Internet Resource Center as you begin a new project. To do so, access the EMC/Paradigm Publishing Web site at www.emcp.com. Click College Division and then under the Quick Links listed at the right of the window, click Internet Resource Centers. Then, under the heading of Computer Applications, click *Integrated Computer Projects*, then Student, and then Student Data Files. The page that displays provides instructions for downloading the data files. Note that the files are organized into folders for each client's projects. Thus, the files for all jobs within a project are included in one folder (for example, client 1 project 1).

Project and Job Scenarios

The following overviews provide a quick reference to the jobs you will complete for each client.

Client 1

International Travel Services (ITS) has franchised travel agencies in 39 states. The agency outsources many specialized technology services to save money and concentrate on its primary business—providing travel services and support for travel agencies.

Job	Description
C1P1J1	You will prepare a letter to respond to a request from ITS for additional information about upgrading to the latest version of Microsoft Office. Some components and a partially written letter will be provided, but an Internet search will be needed to supply additional features to complete the letter.
C1P1J2	A table will be prepared to provide feature comparisons between components of Microsoft Office versions so that ITS can make a more intelligent buying decision. The Internet will be used to determine available components.
C1P1J3	ITS needs pricing information to make a more informed decision about software purchases for its 39 offices. A workbook, with chart, will be provided as input for making good software purchase decisions.
C1P1J4	The manager at ITS decides to recommend purchase of a Microsoft Office Suite. However, a personalized slide presentation is needed to use during an upcoming directors meeting. You will add an appropriate layout, color scheme, transition effects, and preset animation features to the PowerPoint presentation.
C1P1J5	Ronald Powell has been invited to meet with ITS personnel in their home office in New York. You will use Internet resources to make travel plans (airplane, hotel, etc.) and develop a budget for the trip.
C1P1J6	A billing is prepared for services that have been provided to ITS. Workbook data will be summarized and embedded into a short letter that will be composed to transmit the billing information to ITS.
C1P2J1	You will prepare a presentation that includes information about ski lodges that can be placed in agency offices to provide information about travel destinations. You will use the Internet to research information about ten leading ski lodges that will help prepare the presentation. An animated bullet list, graphics, and layout will make an attractive presentation.
C1P2J2	You will develop a Web page containing hyperlinks to the ten ski lodges.
C1P3J1	ITS collected data and placed it in workbooks, but it is not in a useful format. You will prepare appropriate charts and perform data analysis to provide information that will be more useful to the company.
C1P3J2	You will use a partially completed travel pattern report as a foundation for adding charts, footers, layout enhancements, clip art, and other features to provide the two-page report that is needed by the board of directors. Charts that were previously prepared will be incorporated into the report.
C1P4J1	You will use the Internet to determine locations for winter travel events and prepare a workbook, import it into Word and also save it in HTML format.
C1P4J2	You will use enhancements such as WordArt, clip art, text boxes, AutoShape, drawing tools, and other features to prepare a map graphic that will appear in both Word and Web formats showing locations for selected winter travel events.
C1P5J1	You will design a database of screen reports about movies that the clients of ITS agencies can access.

Client 2

Athletic House Sports Center (AHSC) owns full-service health and fitness facilities in 17 locations throughout California, Arizona, and Nevada. The firm often uses BTC's services for activities such as developing promotional literature, maintaining membership lists, and so forth.

Job	Description
C2P1J1	You will assist with preparation of a form letter with mail-merge variables from a workbook to prepare mailing labels for a membership drive. An article will be provided that includes information about fitness program benefits that can be incorporated into a customized letter with a watermark.
C2P1J2	You will revise an outdated membership form. Enhancements and better design concepts will produce a form that may be placed on the AHSC Web site.
C2P1J3	You will compose a three-paragraph form letter and prepare mailing labels for persons who participated in the recent membership recruitment campaign.
C2P2J1	AHSC often receives questions from members. You will use Internet tools to locate appropriate answers to ten questions and then prepare a table for a question-and-answer section on the AHSC Web site. Hyperlinks, AutoFormat, and the company logo will be used to develop an attractive Web page for the company site.
C2P3J1	AHSC personnel developed text for a weekly newsletter, but they need help with design, format, layout, graphics, fonts, and other enhancements to give the newsletter a more professional appearance. Endnotes and a two-column layout are specified.
C2P4J1	You will use a database to perform activities relating to a membership list for the fitness center. Additions, deletions, and revisions will be required.
C2P4J2	AHSC needs a template that can be used to compute and print membership receipts. Formulas, table lookup, macros, and formatting will be used to provide a template form that will be useful and attractive.
C2P5J1	You will use an Outlook calendar to schedule appointments, monitor progress on projects, indicate deadlines, and post reminders. You will record and print calendar information relating to upcoming activities and events.
C2P6J1	You will develop and format a questionnaire to use for determining client interest in the cybercafe concept. You will then use the questionnaire to collect data for analysis and charts to use while preparing a short report on the study results. A sound file will be included in the questionnaire file.
C2P7J1	Using text from a Word document, you will create an interactive slide presentation with hyperlinks, multimedia, animation, graphics, and design effects for an upcoming World Fitness Expo in Phoenix. You will also add 3D WordArt and multimedia action buttons. Transition and build effects will be used to further enhance the presentation.
C2P7J2	The presentation that was created in the previous job for AHSC will be further updated with additional multimedia features for use during the Expo. Audio files, video files, a text box control field, enhanced graphic images, and rehearsed timings will make the presentation more effective.

Client 3

State Community College Association (SCCA) represents community colleges and vocational training schools in the Midwest with more than 344,000 students. The organization relies on BTC to provide services relating to career opportunities for graduates, educational projects, literature development, survey evaluations, fund-raising campaigns, faculty development, and other areas.

Job	Description
C3P1J1	You will use the Internet as a tool for locating information about successful community college graduates. Information about each of 15 persons and a hyperlink to the college attended will be used to develop a workbook that can be posted on the Web site or included in a Word document.
C3P1J2	You will develop an attractive letterhead for SCCA.
C3P1J3	You will develop and implement a mail-merge process for a fund-raising campaign.
C3P1J4	SCCA has job and career information in a document format that must be exported or copied to a workbook format for their purposes. They request many layout and formatting enhancements to make it attractive and functional.
C3P2J1	You will be given a file containing text for an important presentation to be made during an upcoming conference in Hawaii. You will format the paper according to specific guidelines that are provided by the conference director.
C3P3J1	SCCA needs a cover page for an upcoming conference in Seattle. You have been requested to provide three design alternatives. The association will then choose the best design.
C3P4J1	SCCA collected data about reasons employers choose community-college graduates for workforce training. You will analyze and chart the data and then compose a short narrative to describe the results.
C3P5J1	SCCA provides files containing data relating to enrollment projections for community colleges that will be presented to the board of directors. The association requested that charts be developed with a narrative provided to introduce and describe each chart.
C3P6J1	You have been asked to develop two prototypes for electronic grade books to assist faculty with evaluating test scores and determining grades.
C3P6J2	Formulas to determine the course average and a lookup table to determine the final grade need to be added to the gradebooks created in the previous job.
C3P6J3	SCCA has student and advisor data in workbook files. They request that you create a database and then export the Excel data to the database. You are requested to develop a diagram to show the relationship between students and advisors.
C3P6J4	You are requested to perform several queries using the database from the previous job and provide a report for each query.
C3P7J1	SCCA needs help with updating and revising its organizational chart. You will revise the chart, make additions to it, and add enhancements to make the chart more attractive.
C3P8J1	SCCA needs a database to facilitate report creation. Customized reports relating to advisors and students will be developed.

Client 4

Runyan Management Services (RMS) is a privately held company that leases and manages office buildings in seven states with the home office in Boston. The company depends on BTC's extensive graphic arts expertise to design document layouts and develop forms to project a positive image as an industry leader. Tony Burdette, BTC's graphic arts design specialist, will assist with recommendations for several projects.

Job	Description
C4P1J1	**RMS requested development of a form that can be used for recording employee travel expenses. Several formatting adjustments and computations are needed to make the form both attractive and functional.**
C4P1J2	An internal template form to automatically compute commissions, lease income, and other amounts will be developed. The problem format and environment require careful planning and attention to detail. Several enhancements will be added to the form.
C4P1J3	**RMS developed a basic lease availability form, but extensive enhancements are needed to complete the form. This form also requires considerable care to assure that clip art images, font sizes and types, image locations, text boxes, and other formatting design and layout tools are correctly used.**
C4P2J1	This job requires extensive merging of variables to create customized lease and work letter agreement forms. Workbook adjustments to accommodate the variables will also be required. A small amount of editing and formatting is needed as well.
C4P2J2	**A workbook is needed to permit RMS clients to determine periodic lease payments that are required over a long period of time, such as 20 years, based on the installment amount and rate of increase. A user-friendly and attractive form is needed since the workbook may be used in offices or on the company Web site.**
C4P3J1	A transaction timeline is needed for use with project and time management. RMS developed a partially completed timeline. This timeline and other provided information must be carefully studied to complete this project. Detail and layout design are critical components for completion of this project.
C4P4J1	**RMS provided text for an office-building market brief that is not very attractive. Formatting, clip art, and chart development are needed to make an effective document. Arrangement of text, tables, and charts is also important.**
C4P5J1	You will develop a sales flyer template. Planning is critical to assure that clip art images, pictures, text boxes and other elements needed for the flyer are in appropriate colors, locations, and sizes. Layout sheets that are provided with the project will be helpful planning tools.
C4P5J2	**You will develop a rental flyer template. Planning is critical to assure that clip art images, pictures, text boxes and other elements needed for the flyer are in appropriate colors, locations, and sizes. Layout sheets that are provided with the project will be helpful planning tools.**
C4P6J1	RMS requests extensive revisions to an existing presentation. A workbook will be incorporated into one of the slides. Chart creation and layout will be parts of slide development. You will also embed a Flash multimedia movie into the final slide. Instructions are provided to aid in this process.
C4P7J1	**RMS requests extensive revisions to an existing presentation. Several additions, revisions, deletions and enhancements will be required to complete this project. Some slides contain errors that must be detected and corrected.**
C4P8J1	You will adjust properties in an Access database and then prepare a customized form and report. The database will then be exported to an Excel workbook.

Client 5

First South Bank (FSB) is located in New Orleans and offers financial services throughout its region to member banks. BTC helps FSB with many computational and design layouts. FSB has found that services provided by BTC reduce the need for specialized personnel and provide a quicker turnaround time for applications relating to Microsoft Office.

Job	Description
C5P1J1	**A workbook form is needed that provides hyperlinks to banking-related agencies. The workbook will be posted on the bank's Web site. You will use the Internet to locate hyperlinks.**
C5P2J1	A template is needed that will compute interest-related information under each of two assumptions: (1) Periodic payments are made on the loan. (2) The loan amount due is paid in one payment. Formatting will make the template appropriate for posting on the Web site. You will test the template with sample data.
C5P3J1	**A template is needed to determine employee salaries after possible raise factors are considered. The formula used to compute the raise must evaluate the code that determines if an employee will receive a raise. Several function formulas are used with this template.**
C5P4J1	A tutorial has been developed by the Help Desk to assist employees when using the e-mail facility with Outlook. You will test the tutorial to be sure that it is accurate for the latest software version and then format the tutorial for posting on a Web site.
C5P5J1	**RMS requested a workbook containing a loan calculator for posting on its Web site. You will use a template that is available with Microsoft Excel to provide additional formatting and testing to meet company needs.**
C5P6J1	RMS needs a workbook that can be used on mobile and wireless devices to compute securities maturity dates and values. You will revise a partially completed workbook that was provided by RMS to provide an attractive and functional design that includes appropriate formulas. You will also test the workbook with sample data before sending it to RMS.
C5P7J1	**Finance specialists at RMS need to locate financial information from Internet sources while working with an Excel workbook. They must locate information about currency rates, stock quotes, and stock indices on a real-time basis. You will determine how this process is performed and then provide RMS with a tutorial describing the process.**
C5P8J1	Goal seeking is an important workbook function for making projections during the budgeting process. You will develop and test a model that performs this function. Absolute cell addressing is important for this job.
C5P9J1	**RMS needs an enhanced three-panel (two-sided) brochure describing its new college savings program.**
C5P10J1	You will develop a formula for an Excel worksheet on investment bonds, import the files into an Access database, and use the data to prepare a report.
C5P11J1	**The final project is very appropriate as a reward for the expertise that you developed while completing integrated projects for BTC. You will use a wizard (or template) to prepare a résumé for a possible opportunity for promotion. Wizards are useful for completion of many Internet and computer activities.**

International Travel Services
Projects Overview

International Travel Services
1245 Broadway Terrace • New York, NY 10040

International Travel Services (ITS) has franchised travel agencies in 39 states. Three years ago, the company made a decision that many of its specialized information technology needs could best be outsourced to save money, permitting the firm to focus on its primary business—furnishing travel services and support to its franchised travel agencies. Business Technology Consultants (BTC) provides many services to the company.

ITS supports the travel industry with reliable, accurate access to inventory, scheduling, and pricing information. The company is a leading provider of electronic global communications with connections to all major airlines, 40 car rental companies, 47,000 hotel properties, 370 tour operators, and all major cruise lines throughout the world.

Travel agents representing the organization sell the firm's tours, cruises, and independent travel (escorted individuals and groups). The retail division also manages commercial travel accounts of companies under exclusive contracts. The ITS motto is: "Your next trip is never more than a phone call or mouse click away."

The company's mission statement includes four elements:

➢ To fairly compete with other major travel agencies in the areas served by company-owned and franchised travel agencies.
➢ To provide personal and competitive services to clients who visit or contact an agency seeking travel advice.
➢ To provide the best service and quickest response time possible to customers who contact the Web site.
➢ To use current technology and an experienced staff to benefit all travelers.

Services Requested

Ronald Powell has consulted with ITS for three years and is familiar with its operations. He often works with Rhonda Perez, the ITS agency services manager. Currently, he is consulting with her on five projects:

• **Project 1** (six jobs) relates to an application software upgrade ITS is considering. Ronald's assignment is to gather information and create presentation materials Rhonda can share with the board of directors, who will make the final upgrade

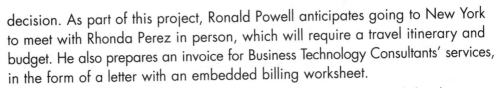

decision. As part of this project, Ronald Powell anticipates going to New York to meet with Rhonda Perez in person, which will require a travel itinerary and budget. He also prepares an invoice for Business Technology Consultants' services, in the form of a letter with an embedded billing worksheet.

- **Project 2** (two jobs) involves preparing a slide presentation and developing a Web page featuring U.S. ski resorts.
- **Project 3** (two jobs) requires creating a workbook of tables and charts along with a written report analyzing data on domestic travel volume.
- **Project 4** (two jobs) calls for creating documents in several formats that ITS can use to promote its winter vacation packages in print and on the Web.
- **Project 5** (one job) implements a database design to create screen reports while using business rules for tables and attributes relating to movie information.

Business Technology Consultants
Project and Job Information

Client: International Travel Services   Project: p1j1

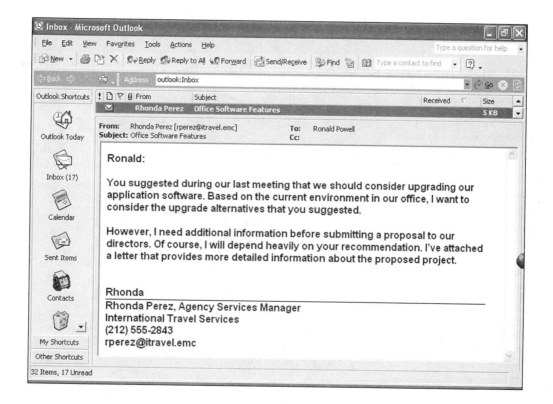

Client: _____International Travel Services_____ Project: _____p1j1_____

International Travel Services
1245 Broadway Terrace • New York, NY 10040

Rhonda Perez
Agency Services Manager
(212) 555-2843

April 23, 200X

Mr. Ronald Powell, Chief Consultant
Business Technology Consultants
1122 Peachtree Hills Avenue
Atlanta, GA 30306

Dear Ronald:

Thank you for the feasibility study that you provided to support our recent purchase of software, microcomputers, and a file server for our new intranet. Your training classes for our end users were very helpful prior to the implementation process.

You also suggested that we consider a move to the latest version of Microsoft Office application software to take advantage of its Web, multimedia, and collaboration capabilities. A local community college seminar I attended supported your ideas about this upgrade. Our board of directors will make the final upgrade decision. I need a letter from you to distribute at the upcoming board meeting that describes typical features you feel will be beneficial for applications at our company. A separate list comparing the software components of the two upgrades you are recommending will also be useful, along with a spreadsheet and bar chart showing the costs of the two upgrades as well as those costs we would incur if we opted to purchase individual software packages for each employee. I will also need a supporting slide presentation I can present at the directors' meeting.

I hope BTC will be available and interested in providing training for end users if the proposal to upgrade software is approved. Please let me know by early next week whether you will be able to provide these services.

Sincerely,

Rhonda Perez
Agency Services Manager

Client: _____International Travel Services_____ Project: _____p1j1_____

Job #1

Files Needed
upgrade.doc

Below is the rough draft of the letter Rhonda Perez needs for her board. Based on a follow-up call, she wants to include seven features for the proposed upgrade. Conduct an Internet search to find information on features of the newest Office upgrade. Select two to add to the list in the letter. Use checkmark bullets for the list. Rhonda needs this letter as soon as possible.

Thank you for your recent request for additional information about the new Microsoft Office upgrade. There are several benefits in upgrading to the latest version. Major features of this version include:

smart tags to provide speedy access to relevant information
task panes to provide quick access to files and formatting tools
an added data feature for gathering information from the Web
document recovery to automatically save documents when the computer stops responding
speech recognition to permit entering of text and/or navigating menus

You asked whether your company should consider the Office Professional Edition, the Office Professional Special Edition, or individual software programs for your employees. The enclosed table illustrates the major components of each of the two Office versions. You will also find enclosed an Excel spreadsheet that illustrates potential pricing patterns, including those for individual programs. With your large number of users, you will probably want to consider a suite price or a licensing program.

If you decide to upgrade to the latest version of Office, our company will be happy to quote a price for your training program to help end users move efficiently to the new version.

Sincerely,

Ronald Powell
Chief Consultant

Enclosures

Job Planning Form

Client: _____ Project: _____ Job: _____

1. What deliverables does the client expect for this job? (Examples include letter, printed report, slide presentation, database file, template, spreadsheet.)

2. Which additional resources, if any, do you need in finding information to complete the job? (Examples include Internet searches and documents on disk.)

3. What software do you need to complete this job?

4. What special software formatting features does the job call for?

STUDENT LOG

Name: _____ Date/Time Completed: _____

Document File Name(s): _____

Comments:

Client: _International Travel Services_   Project: _p1j2_

Job #2

Files Needed
None

The following draft table includes a partial list of software components that are included in two of the Office suite software versions Ronald Powell has recommended for International Travel Services. Find out the names of the two editions of Microsoft® Office and verify that the components are correct as listed. Then create a table that includes a complete listing of the software components for the two versions. Rhonda Perez wants a table that is attractively designed and formatted. Print a copy of the table, which will be sent to Rhonda.

→ Standard
Professional

Office Suite Software Components
Prepared for Ms. Rhonda Perez, Agency Services Manager
International Travel Services

Word	Word
Excel	Excel
Outlook	Outlook
PowerPoint	
Access	

Business Technology Consultants

Client: _____ Project: _____ Job: _____

1. What deliverables does the client expect for this job? (Examples include letter, printed report, slide presentation, database file, template, spreadsheet.)

2. Which additional resources, if any, do you need in finding information to complete the job? (Examples include Internet searches and documents on disk.)

3. What software do you need to complete this job?

4. What special software formatting features does the job call for?

STUDENT LOG

Name: _____ Date/Time Completed: _____

Document File Name(s): _____

Comments:

Client: _____ International Travel Services _____ Project: _____ p1j3 _____

Job #3

Files Needed
None

Rhonda Perez needs information about whether to purchase *standard* software as (1) Office Professional Edition, (2) Office Professional Special Edition, or (3) individual programs for all 629 employees. The table below shows recent software prices. Rhonda will need a ~~workbook~~ spreadsheet ~~showing~~ *Excel* costs for each of the three options and also a bar chart to show a three-way price comparison. A ~~chart~~ legend would be helpful. She wants a spreadsheet design that is attractive and functional—~~with color,~~ ~~centered main and column headings,~~ and so forth. Data in a previous job indicates components that are included in each suite.

Estimated Software Upgrade Cost
Prepared for Ms. Rhonda Perez, Agency Services Manager
International Travel Services

Software Program	Number of Units	Cost Per Unit	Total Cost
Office Suite Professional *Standard*	629	$ 364.75	
Office ~~Suite Special Edition~~	629	479.50	
Word	629	99.25	
Excel	629	99.25	
Access	325	119.25	
Outlook	629	79.50	
PowerPoint	415	99.25	
Visio *Standard*	18	110.75	
Publisher	18	99.95	

Old Price

Job Planning Form • • •

Client: _____ Project: _____ Job: _____

1. What deliverables does the client expect for this job? (Examples include letter, printed report, slide presentation, database file, template, spreadsheet.)

2. Which additional resources, if any, do you need in finding information to complete the job? (Examples include Internet searches and documents on disk.)

3. What software do you need to complete this job?

4. What special software formatting features does the job call for?

STUDENT LOG

Name: _____ Date/Time Completed: _____

Document File Name(s): _____

Comments:

Client: **International Travel Services** Project: **p1j4**

Job #4

Files Needed
None

Rhonda Perez needs a slide presentation highlighting the features of the two Office upgrades. In a phone conversation, she asked Ronald Powell to incorporate an appropriate layout and color scheme along with transition effects. Following the phone call, Rhonda sent this e-mail.

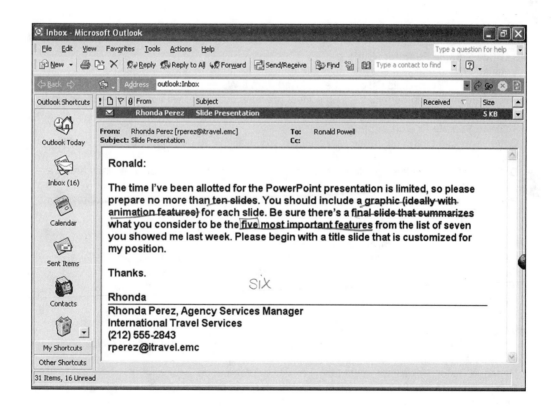

Client: ___International Travel Services___ Project: ____p1j4____

Job #4

(continued)
Files Needed
None

Rhonda approved the following list of features, tentatively grouped to fit on five slides. She and Ronald agreed that each item featured in the slide presentation must fit onto a single line, so some editing will be necessary. The final printed copy of the presentation should have six slides per page.

MS Office Sample Features, Slide 1
- Settings Wizard makes it easy to save and recreate settings on another machine.
- Setup from HTTP permits Office to be installed from a Web server.
- Document versioning permits tracking so that previous document versions can be retrieved.

MS Office Sample Features, Slide 2
- Documents can be stored on the server and made available to others to view only, if editing is not desired.
- Draft copies can be stored in a way that they are not accessible by others until they are in a publishable form.
- Publishing Approval feature allows users to establish easy procedures to obtain approval for publishing a document.

MS Office Sample Features, Slide 3
- File formats are backward compatible to previous Office software versions.
- Office Clipboard allows users to copy up to 24 pieces of information at once.
- The Office Assistant is hidden by default. It appears only when Help is activated.
- Excel data can be refreshed from the Web.

MS Office Sample Features, Slide 4
- Print from Browser feature allows users to print an HTML file from the original Office document in which it was created.
- Hyperlink Dialog Box allows users to link to files in Web pages.
- Compare and Merge feature allows the user to merge comments and revisions from multiple reviewers. The author can accept or reject one or all revisions.

MS Office Sample Features, Slide 5
- Custom Installation Wizard has been improved to permit previous version files to be removed at the time of installation.
- International Support feature provides the product in more languages—26 for FrontPage.

Job Planning Form

Client: _____ Project: _____ Job: _____

1. What deliverables does the client expect for this job? (Examples include letter, printed report, slide presentation, database file, template, spreadsheet.)

2. Which additional resources, if any, do you need in finding information to complete the job? (Examples include Internet searches and documents on disk.)

3. What software do you need to complete this job?

4. What special software formatting features does the job call for?

STUDENT LOG

Name: _____ Date/Time Completed: _____

Document File Name(s): _____

Comments:

Client: _____ International Travel Services _____ Project: _____ p1j5 _____

Job #5

Files Needed
None

Ronald Powell needs a professionally formatted travel itinerary and budget for a trip to visit Rhonda Perez in New York. His tentative plan is to fly out of Atlanta on the second Monday of next month and return on Wednesday of the same week. Travel costs will include airfare, meals, car rental, airport parking, and hotel. Ronald prefers to stay in Manhattan. ITS will reimburse meal costs of up to $100 per day. If possible, keep the total cost of the trip to $1,500 or less. The following URLs offer a starting point for your travel research:

- http://msn.expedia.com
- http://www.nwa.com
- http://www.nationalcar.com
- http://gmvacations.com

Job Planning Form

Client: _____ Project: _____ Job: _____

1. What deliverables does the client expect for this job? (Examples include letter, printed report, slide presentation, database file, template, spreadsheet.)

2. Which additional resources, if any, do you need in finding information to complete the job? (Examples include Internet searches and documents on disk.)

3. What software do you need to complete this job?

4. What special software formatting features does the job call for?

STUDENT LOG

Name: _____ Date/Time Completed: _____

Document File Name(s): _____

Comments:

Client: _International Travel Services_   Project: _p1j6_

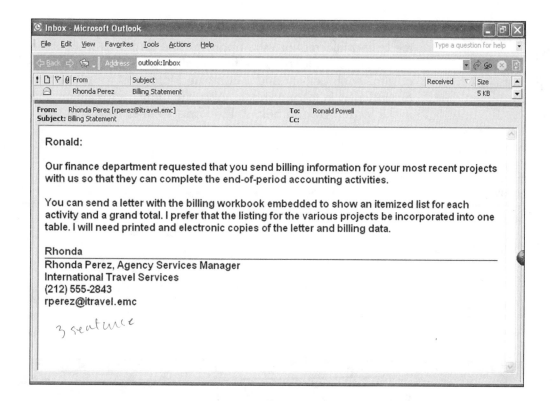

Client: **International Travel Services**   Project: **p1j6**

Job #6

NOTES

Files Needed
billing.xls

The letter to Rhonda Perez should be three paragraphs long. For the billing information, she approved the format at the bottom of this page, as long as the formulas needed to compute a total cost for each activity and a combined total cost for all activities are included in the workbook. Write the formulas for the activities in the form provided below. Then add them to the Excel file.

Activity 1:	
Activity 2:	
Activity 3:	
Activity 4:	
Activity 5:	
Activity 6:	
Grand Total:	

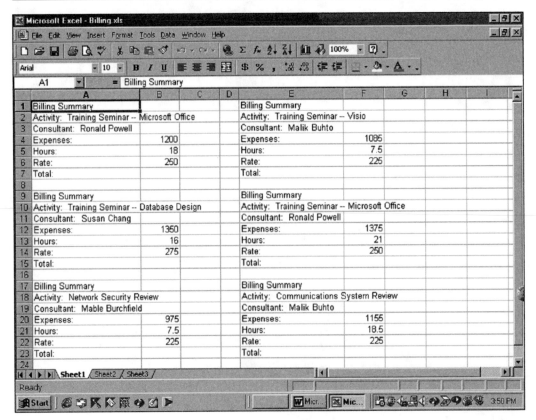

Business Technology Consultants

Client: _____ Project: _____ Job: _____

1. What deliverables does the client expect for this job? (Examples include letter, printed report, slide presentation, database file, template, spreadsheet.)

2. Which additional resources, if any, do you need in finding information to complete the job? (Examples include Internet searches and documents on disk.)

3. What software do you need to complete this job?

4. What special software formatting features does the job call for?

STUDENT LOG

Name: _____ Date/Time Completed: _____

Document File Name(s): _____

Comments:

Business Technology Consultants
Project and Job Information

Client: _____International Travel Services_____ Project: _____p2j1_____

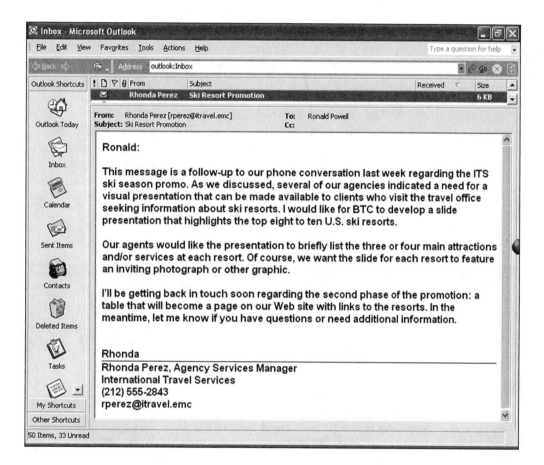

Client: ___International Travel Services___ Project: ___p2j1___

Job #1

Files Needed
income.xls

The information in the graphic below provides a starting point for this job. Rhonda Perez requested that a template be selected and applied for the entire slide presentation. She wants a title slide, one slide for each of the ten resorts (to include a graphic and three-item animated bulleted list; find information for the bullets at the resort Web sites), a slide that shows sources of agency income from the income.xls workbook, and a closing slide with a graphic. Images for the slides can be downloaded from appropriate Web sites, as long as copyright laws are not violated. Set the presentation to advance to a new slide after ten-second intervals.

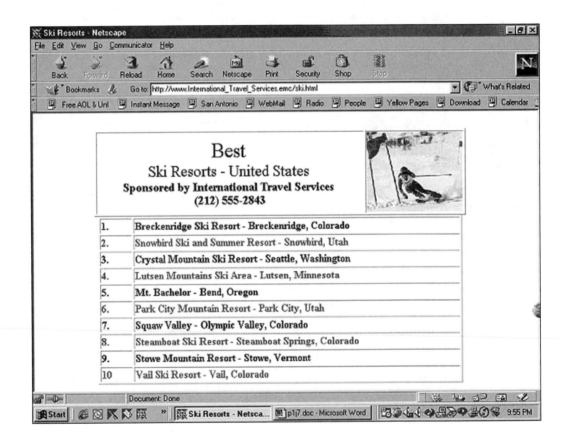

Job Planning Form

Client: _____ Project:_____ Job: _____

1. What deliverables does the client expect for this job? (Examples include letter, printed report, slide presentation, database file, template, spreadsheet.)

2. Which additional resources, if any, do you need in finding information to complete the job? (Examples include Internet searches and documents on disk.)

3. What software do you need to complete this job?

4. What special software formatting features does the job call for?

STUDENT LOG

Name: _____ Date/Time Completed: _____

Document File Name(s): _____

Comments:

Business Technology Consultants

Business Technology Consultants
Project and Job Information

Client: _____ International Travel Services _____ Project: _____ p2j2 _____

Job #2

Files Needed
ski.html

Rhonda Perez called Ronald Powell to discuss the second phase of the promotion. ITS plans to include a page on its Web site promoting the top ten U.S. ski resorts. On the page, Rhonda wants a three-column table that includes each resort's number rank, its name and location, and a link to its home page so clients can find additional information. Below is the preliminary design for the Web page. Revise it as a Word document and then create a new Web page, using a program such as FrontPage.

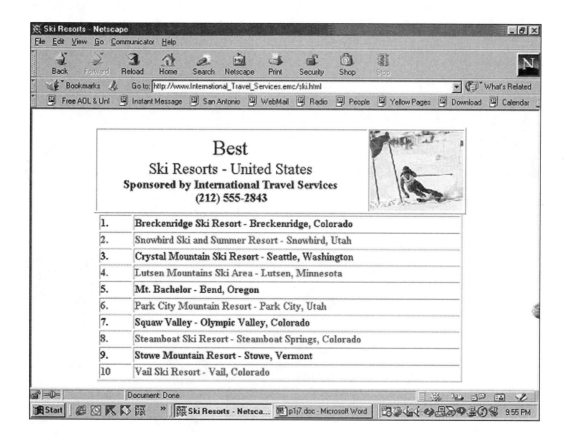

• • • Job Planning Form • • •

Client: _____ Project: _____ Job: _____

1. What deliverables does the client expect for this job? (Examples include letter, printed report, slide presentation, database file, template, spreadsheet.)

2. Which additional resources, if any, do you need in finding information to complete the job? (Examples include Internet searches and documents on disk.)

3. What software do you need to complete this job?

4. What special software formatting features does the job call for?

STUDENT LOG

Name: _____ Date/Time Completed: _____

Document File Name(s): _____

Comments:

Client: **International Travel Services** Project: **p3j1**

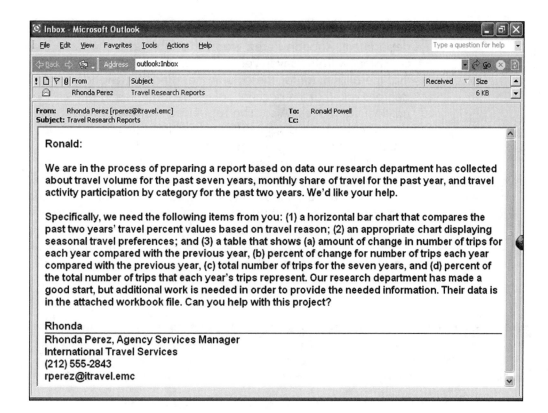

Inbox - Microsoft Outlook

File Edit View Favorites Tools Actions Help   Type a question for help

Back   Address outlook:Inbox   Go

! D ∇ θ From   Subject   Received ▽ Size
  Rhonda Perez   Travel Research Reports   6 KB

From: Rhonda Perez [rperez@itravel.emc]   To: Ronald Powell
Subject: Travel Research Reports   Cc:

Ronald:

We are in the process of preparing a report based on data our research department has collected about travel volume for the past seven years, monthly share of travel for the past year, and travel activity participation by category for the past two years. We'd like your help.

Specifically, we need the following items from you: (1) a horizontal bar chart that compares the past two years' travel percent values based on travel reason; (2) an appropriate chart displaying seasonal travel preferences; and (3) a table that shows (a) amount of change in number of trips for each year compared with the previous year, (b) percent of change for number of trips each year compared with the previous year, (c) total number of trips for the seven years, and (d) percent of the total number of trips that each year's trips represent. Our research department has made a good start, but additional work is needed in order to provide the needed information. Their data is in the attached workbook file. Can you help with this project?

Rhonda
Rhonda Perez, Agency Services Manager
International Travel Services
(212) 555-2843
rperez@itravel.emc

Client: **International Travel Services**   Project: **p3j1**

Job #1

Files Needed
travel_reasons.xls

Below is a table from the spreadsheet created by the ITS research department. Rhonda Perez wants this table formatted in a style consistent with the seven-year table on the next page. She asked that the alignment for the column headings be changed to ten degrees and that the decimal values be formatted to percents with no decimal places. Also, she requested that the figures in the Year 2 column be displayed in a blue boldface font for each instance where the Year 2 percent is larger than the Year 1 percent. It will be necessary to change the Year headings to actual years (two years ago for Year 1, one year ago for Year 2).

Once the table is finished, create a horizontal bar chart comparing the percent values for the two years relative to each category and label the percents at the end of each bar. Rhonda wants the name of each category to the left of the appropriate bar. Include a title with the chart.

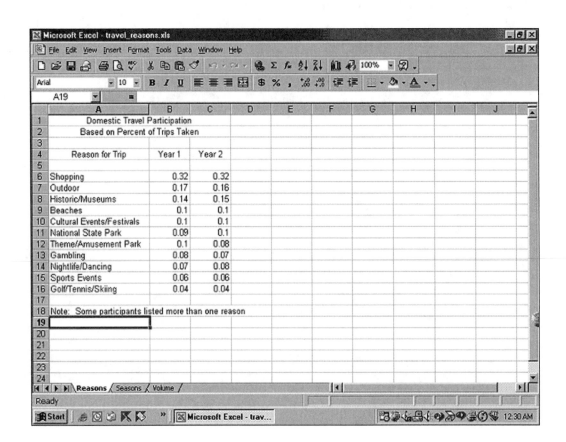

	Reason for Trip	Year 1	Year 2
	Domestic Travel Participation		
	Based on Percent of Trips Taken		
6	Shopping	0.32	0.32
7	Outdoor	0.17	0.16
8	Historic/Museums	0.14	0.15
9	Beaches	0.1	0.1
10	Cultural Events/Festivals	0.1	0.1
11	National State Park	0.09	0.1
12	Theme/Amusement Park	0.1	0.08
13	Gambling	0.08	0.07
14	Nightlife/Dancing	0.07	0.08
15	Sports Events	0.06	0.06
16	Golf/Tennis/Skiing	0.04	0.04
18	Note: Some participants listed more than one reason		

Client: **International Travel Services** Project: **p3j1**

Job #1

(continued)
Files Needed
travel_reasons.xls

Rhonda and Ronald agreed that the data about seasonal travel preferences is to be presented in a pie chart. The slice representing the largest percent is to be exploded to add emphasis to the corresponding season. Include a legend and the percent values to display with the chart.

The seven-year table showing the number of trips per year needs several revisions. Formulas are required for all calculations. The Change column should display the change from the previous year. For example, the Year 2 change will display the change between Year 1 and Year 2. The Year 3 change will display the change between Year 2 and Year 3. The Percent of Change column should display the percent of change from the previous year. Any negative changes should appear inside parentheses. The Percent of Total amount will be determined by a comparison of each year's No. of Trips with the Total. The two-line table heading should be centered across the table, with cells merged; column headings should be centered as well. Rhonda wants a copy of the completed table. She also requested an additional printed copy displaying the table with formulas in case her staff needs to review them.

Seasons for Travel	
Season	**Percent**
Winter	20
Spring	23
Summer	33
Fall	24
Total	100

Domestic Travel Activity Millions of Person Trips				
Year	**No. of Trips**	**Change**	**Percent of Change**	**Percent of Total**
Year 1	931		0	
Year 2	962			
Year 3	971			
Year 4	989			
Year 5	1014			
Year 6	992			
Year 7	996			
Total				

Business
Technology
Consultants

Job Planning Form • • •

Client: _____ Project: _____ Job: _____

1. What deliverables does the client expect for this job? (Examples include letter, printed report, slide presentation, database file, template, spreadsheet.)

2. Which additional resources, if any, do you need in finding information to complete the job? (Examples include Internet searches and documents on disk.)

3. What software do you need to complete this job?

4. What special software formatting features does the job call for?

STUDENT LOG

Name: _____ Date/Time Completed: _____

Document File Name(s): _____

Comments:

Client: **International Travel Services** Project: **p3j2**

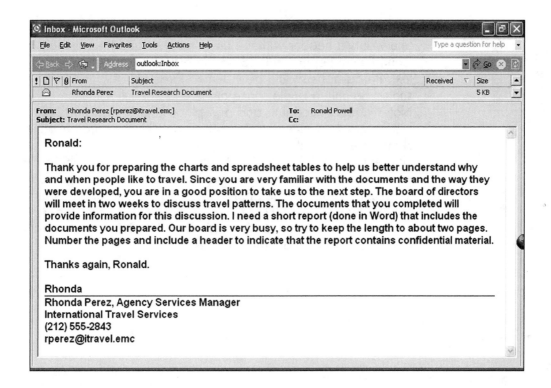

Inbox - Microsoft Outlook

File Edit View Favorites Tools Actions Help   Type a question for help

Back | Address outlook:Inbox   Go

!	From	Subject	Received	Size
	Rhonda Perez	Travel Research Document		5 KB

From: Rhonda Perez [rperez@itravel.emc]   **To:** Ronald Powell
Subject: Travel Research Document   **Cc:**

Ronald:

Thank you for preparing the charts and spreadsheet tables to help us better understand why and when people like to travel. Since you are very familiar with the documents and the way they were developed, you are in a good position to take us to the next step. The board of directors will meet in two weeks to discuss travel patterns. The documents that you completed will provide information for this discussion. I need a short report (done in Word) that includes the documents you prepared. Our board is very busy, so try to keep the length to about two pages. Number the pages and include a header to indicate that the report contains confidential material.

Thanks again, Ronald.

Rhonda
Rhonda Perez, Agency Services Manager
International Travel Services
(212) 555-2843
rperez@itravel.emc

Client: **International Travel Services**   Project: **p3j2**

Job #2

Files Needed
travel_patterns.doc
travel_reasons.xls

Below is a draft of the travel pattern report for Rhonda Perez. She wants a header with the page number and the notation Confidential Report, in bold and in a font different from the text. Paragraphs should be indented three spaces, and there should be only a single space at the end of each sentence. Notes about material to add and placement of the charts are in brackets (<>). Center the visuals horizontally. The report heading should be in boldface and centered horizontally; center the "Presented by" line and give it light gray shading. Include a clip art image at the beginning of the document—something related to travel. Size the image appropriately so that the report requires exactly two pages. Include a page border for both pages. Following the third table (Domestic Travel Activity), add a short discussion of the information it presents.

U. S. Domestic Vacation Travel Patterns
Presented by Ms. Rhonda Perez, Agency Services Manager

Studies have shown that domestic travelers take vacation trips for a variety of purposes ranging from shopping to golf, tennis, and skiing. Based on travel participation for the past two years, reasons for taking trips have not changed, with the following exceptions: **<List the reasons that are not the same for both years.>** A range of reasons travelers cite for taking vacation trips is shown in the following chart.

<Insert the Domestic Travel Participation bar chart here.>

Generally, people seemed to do a similar amount of vacation travel in each season, with the exception of summer, which had higher volumes. Family vacations are normally taken during the summer, so this may account for the summer season claiming the highest percent of travel. Travel during the four seasons is shown in the following chart.

<Insert the Seasons for Travel pie chart here.>

Data were collected to determine the change in travel, as represented by number of trips taken, over the past seven years. The number of trips taken each year was also compared with the total number of trips taken during the period. Domestic travel activity information for the past seven years is shown in the following table.

<Insert the Domestic Travel Activity table here.>

· · · **Job Planning Form** · · ·

Client: _____ Project:_____ Job: _____

1. What deliverables does the client expect for this job? (Examples include letter, printed report, slide presentation, database file, template, spreadsheet.)

2. Which additional resources, if any, do you need in finding information to complete the job? (Examples include Internet searches and documents on disk.)

3. What software do you need to complete this job?

4. What special software formatting features does the job call for?

STUDENT LOG

Name: _____ Date/Time Completed: _____

Document File Name(s): _____

Comments:

Client: _____ International Travel Services _____ Project: _____ p4j1 _____

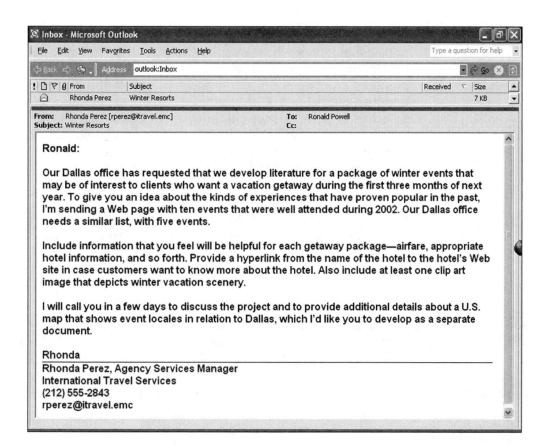

Client: **International Travel Services**   Project: **p4j1**

Job #1

Files Needed
None

On the phone, Rhonda Perez told Ronald Powell she was unsure about what format would work best for the vacation information the Dallas group needs. They decided the document should be prepared as a workbook (attractively formatted and designed), and then copied to a Word format as well. It should also be saved as an HTML document, in case the Dallas agents want to link to it from their Web site. Rhonda wants the workbook to contain columns for the name of the event, event location, event dates, roundtrip airfares from Dallas, and the name of a suggested hotel near the event. Clip art can be downloaded from the Internet as long as copyright laws are not violated. Below is a printout of the Web page Rhonda mentioned in her e-mail. Use Internet search engines to locate five events that should be of interest to ITS clients.

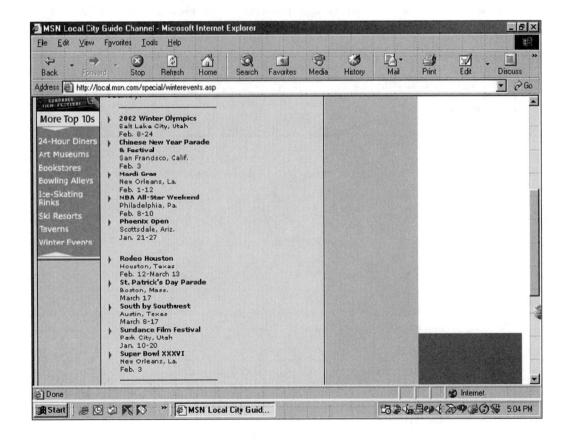

•••• Job Planning Form ••••

Client: _____ Project: _____ Job: _____

1. What deliverables does the client expect for this job? (Examples include letter, printed report, slide presentation, database file, template, spreadsheet.)

2. Which additional resources, if any, do you need in finding information to complete the job? (Examples include Internet searches and documents on disk.)

3. What software do you need to complete this job?

4. What special software formatting features does the job call for?

STUDENT LOG

Name: _____ Date/Time Completed: _____

Document File Name(s): _____

Comments:

Client: _____ International Travel Services _____ Project: _____ p4j2 _____

Job #2

Files Needed
(See next page)

Rhonda Perez wants to provide a map that shows the location of the five events highlighted in the vacation packages information. She sent the following example of a map that uses dots for this purpose. She also liked Ronald Powell's idea of using Microsoft Word's AutoShape feature to create red stars showing the event locations along with a blue line beginning at Dallas and ending at each event city—one line per event.

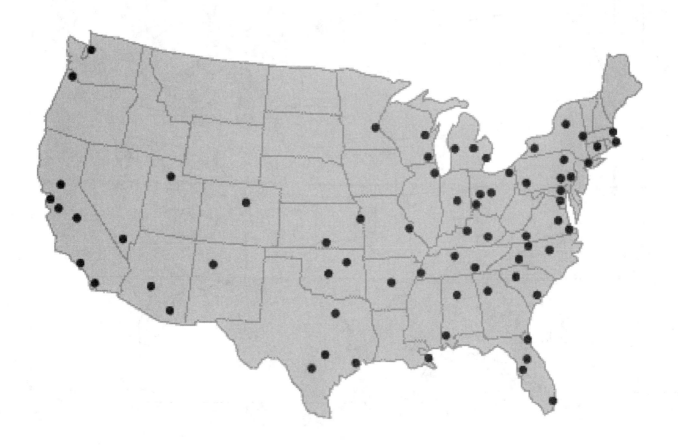

Client: **International Travel Services**   Project: **p4j2**

Job #2

(continued)
Files Needed

map_usa.jpg

Shown below is the map graphic for this job. Use WordArt and drawing tools to add dots and lines to the map. Keep the map document separate from the rest of the package, so agents can e-mail or fax it to clients.

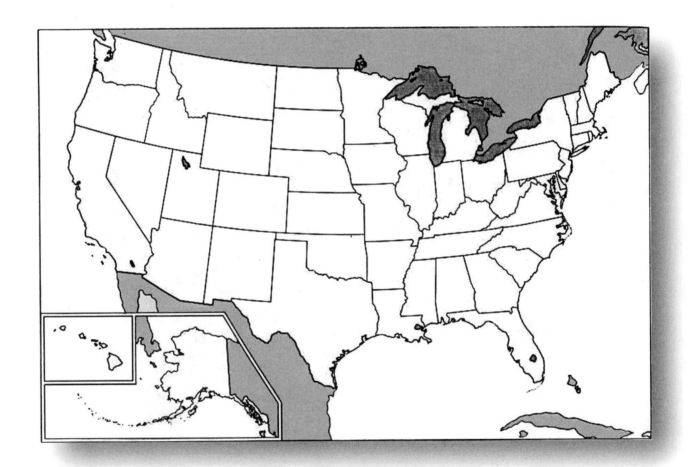

Client: _____ Project: _____ Job: _____

1. What deliverables does the client expect for this job? (Examples include letter, printed report, slide presentation, database file, template, spreadsheet.)

2. Which additional resources, if any, do you need in finding information to complete the job? (Examples include Internet searches and documents on disk.)

3. What software do you need to complete this job?

4. What special software formatting features does the job call for?

STUDENT LOG

Name: _____ Date/Time Completed: _____

Document File Name(s): _____

Comments:

Client: _____International Travel Services_____ Project: _____p5j1_____

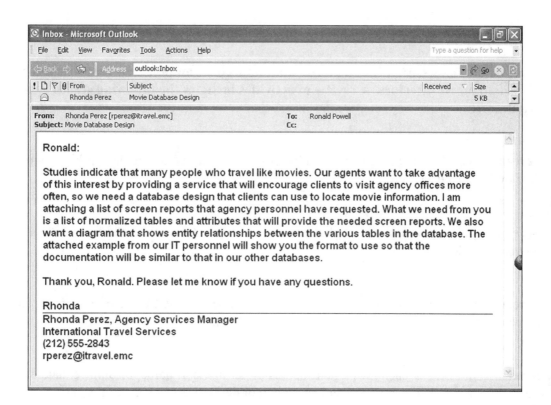

Job #1

Files Needed
None

Text for the files Rhonda Perez attached is shown on the following pages. The business rules for the screen reports provide a basis for determining the relationship that exists between tables. The Web site of The Internet Movie Database (www.imdb.com) is an excellent resource. The database for Rhonda should include information on 20 movies.

Client: _International Travel Services_   Project: _p5j1_

Database Design Screen Reports

A movie database design is needed that maintains information about movies, movie stars, and movie directors. A review of activities includes the following screen report requirements.

Screen Report 1. For each director, list his or her number, name, the date of birth, and date of death (if deceased).

Screen Report 2. For each movie, list its movie number, movie title, and the year that the movie was released.

Screen Report 3. For each movie, list its movie number, movie title, and the number and name of its director.

Screen Report 4. For each movie star, list his or her number, name, birthplace, date of birth, date of death (if deceased), and computed or derived age at time of death (if deceased).

Screen Report 5. For each movie, list its number and movie title, along with the numbers and names of stars appearing in the movie.

Screen Report 6. For each movie star, list his or her number and name along with the number and name of all movies in which he or she starred.

Business Rules

1. Each director can direct more than one movie.
2. Each movie can have more than one director.
3. Each movie star can appear in more than one movie.
4. Each movie can include more than one movie star.

Client: **International Travel Services** Project: **p5j1**

Database Design Considerations
Relations, attributes, and primary keys are represented as follows. Student(ID, Lname, Fname, …)
An asterisk to the right of an attribute indicates that the attribute is permitted to have a null value. A slash to the left of an attribute indicates that it has a derived value.
Alternate keys, if any, are identified by the letters AK and followed by the attribute(s) that comprise the alternate key.
Secondary keys are identified by the letters SK and followed by the attribute(s) that comprise the secondary key.
Foreign keys are identified by the letters FK and followed by the attribute(s) that comprise the foreign key plus the name of the table where the corresponding primary key is located.

The following example illustrates use of key notation for two relations.
 	
Employee(Emp_Num, Emp_Name, Emp_Addr*, SS_Num, Dept_Num, …)
    AK   SS_Num
    SK   Emp_Name
    FK   Dept_Num → Department

The following example illustrates the notation to be used for the entity-relational diagrams. The asterisk (*) is used to indicate "many," a numeral one (1) is used to indicate "one," and a numeral zero (0) is used to indicate "zero" or "optional" in the relationships between tables.

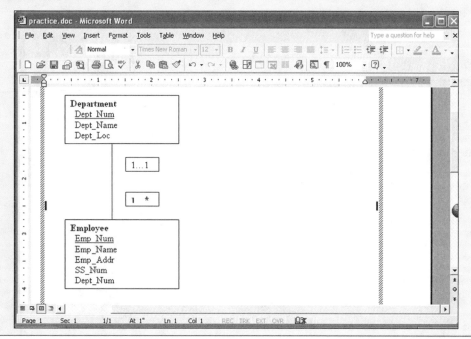

Job Planning Form

Client: _____ Project: _____ Job: _____

1. What deliverables does the client expect for this job? (Examples include letter, printed report, slide presentation, database file, template, spreadsheet.)

2. Which additional resources, if any, do you need in finding information to complete the job? (Examples include Internet searches and documents on disk.)

3. What software do you need to complete this job?

4. What special software formatting features does the job call for?

STUDENT LOG

Name: _____ Date/Time Completed: _____

Document File Name(s): _____

Comments:

Athletic House Sports Center (AHSC) was established in 1986 with the opening of a modern racquetball club. Today, the firm has 17 locations throughout California, Arizona, and Nevada. The company offers a diverse range of programs, services, and activities that cover almost all areas of fitness fun. Each center is open 24 hours a day, seven days a week, to accommodate the schedules and lifestyles of its members. The company also sells a wide variety of athletic equipment and supplies to members and the general public who order from its Web site. Corporate programs are available as well.

AHSC offers a wide selection of classes, from step aerobics to kick boxing, free to members. Every center is equipped with modern equipment to make fitness activities as safe and productive as possible. All instructors at each center have Board of Physical Fitness certification as Certified Personal Trainers. They can provide information on how to balance diet and exercise to help clients keep looking and feeling great. Members can purchase athletic apparel at a 15 percent discount—even for items already on sale.

The vision of the company is to be the best in the industry while partnering with clients to help them enjoy longer, happier, more productive, and healthier lives. The firm states its mission to members in this way: "Helping you become healthier and happier one day at a time." The corporate motto is: "AHSC makes it easy for you to get and stay fit. Do something for yourself today."

Services Requested

Athletic House Sports Center is a client of Business Technology Consultants (BTC), serviced by Ronald Powell. Dr. Frank McKenzie, the AHSC director of operations, is Ronald's main contact. Many of Ronald's consulting services relate to development of promotional materials, maintaining membership lists, maintaining inventory records, and activities in other areas that arise on a periodic basis. Currently, Ronald is consulting with Frank on seven projects:

- **Project 1** (three jobs) calls for BTC to create and test form letters and assist with a membership application form.
- **Project 2** (one job) involves researching information and developing a Web page on sports injuries in a question-and-answer format.

- **Project 3** (one job) is an assignment to design and format AHSC's newsletter.
- **Project 4** (two jobs) relates to adapting and testing the company's interactive membership database.
- **Project 5** (one job) requires creating an electronic business calendar.
- **Project 6** (one job) involves preparing a questionnaire in both Web and print formats.
- **Project 7** (two jobs) is a major update of AHSC's promotional slide show that includes converting it into a multimedia presentation.

Client: **Athletic House Sports Center** Project: **p1j1**

Job #1

Files Needed
roster.xls
roster.doc
logo.bmp

Frank McKenzie wants BTC to develop a form-letter main document that can be sent to prospective customers who have expressed an interest in membership based on a visit, an e-mail message, or a phone call to one of the centers. He sent Ronald Powell a workbook to provide a sample data source to supply variables for the form letter during the mail-merge process. The data can also be used to prepare address labels—Avery 8160 or Avery 5162. Frank wants the labels printed in ascending order based on the zip code.

Along with the data, Frank sent a draft of the form letter and an article that discusses benefits of stretching exercises in a flexible fitness program. The final letter needs to include a bulleted list of six benefits, based on the article; the draft currently includes one of these. The letter, which should be from Dr. McKenzie, should also include the company symbol as a watermark. The address for the main office of the company is 2364 Park Terrace Avenue, Los Angeles, California 93721. The phone number is (323) 555-2222.

A copy of the revised form-letter main document, the seven letters produced during the mail-merge process, and the address labels (printed on a sheet of paper) should provide Frank with everything he needs for this job.

Sample Prospect Roster

Title	Last	First	Street	City	State	Zip
Mr.	Zaner	Jim	835 Jackson	San Fancisco	CA	94133
Ms.	Scott	Jennifer	2014 Tulane	Fresno	CA	93760
Ms.	Padakala	Vandana	225 E. Main	El Cajon	CA	92020
Mr.	Gao	Yuan	1682 Buena Vista	Anaheim	CA	92602
Ms.	Benedito	Mia	300 E. Olive Avenue	Burbank	CA	91502
Mr.	Cotton	Matt	6430 W. Sunset Boulevard	Los Angeles	CA	90026
Mr.	Green	Caleb	10447 La Conta Avenue	Los Angeles	CA	90024

Client: _____Athletic House Sports Center_____ Project: _____p1j1_____

Draft of Form Letter

<Current date here>

<Address variables here>

Dear **<Title variable here> <Last name variable here>**:

Thank you for your interest in our fitness program. "AHSC makes it easy for you to get and stay fit. Do something for yourself today." This is our motto. With a team effort between you and our personal trainers, this motto will become a goal that is within your reach.

You requested information about the benefits of stretching exercises as part of the total fitness program. Benefits of stretching include the following:

• It lowers the risk of injury and improves physical performance.

A copy of our enrollment application is enclosed. You'll want to return the form as soon as possible so you can get started on your fitness program. If you have questions, please let me know.

<Closing lines here>

Client: __Athletic House Sports Center__ Project: ___p1j1___

Article

Benefits of Stretching in Flexible Fitness Training
By Dr. Ashley Hicks

A routine of physical activity that includes stretching exercises can provide greater flexibility for the fitness training program. Flexibility is important to improve a joint's ability to move through a full range of motion.

Along with physical activity, stretching will improve the body's ability to increase physical performance in day-to-day activities. A stronger muscle group also makes the body less prone to routine injuries.

Muscle soreness will be less likely with slow stretching activities. Stretching also improves body posture in activities performed on a daily basis. A stretch should be held for 15 to 30 seconds to be most effective.

Stretching encourages the muscles to relax. Stretching the hamstrings, hip flexors, quadriceps, and other muscles attaching to the pelvis can reduce the potential for muscle shortening or tightening and thus reduce fatigue. This process will result in less pressure on the lower back. Persons who perform stretching exercises at least three times a week are less likely to exhibit symptoms that lead to lower back pain.

Another great benefit is that stretching increases blood supply and nutrients to joint structures and the supply of blood throughout the body. Stretching also increases joint fluids, which promotes the transport of more nutrients to the joint's cartilage. This process permits a greater range of motion and reduces joint degeneration of the muscle tissue that surrounds the bones in the body.

Stretching can also increase neuromuscular coordination to reduce the time it takes an impulse to travel to the brain and back. Muscle groups are then able to work in a more synergistic, coordinated fashion, which improves performance of activities.

A fitness program can be fun and relaxing for both mind and body. Working with a personal trainer can also provide encouragement and increase performance. A successful program helps make a person have a positive attitude about daily activities. Without flexibility training, an important part of overall health is missed.

Business
Technology
Consultants

Job Planning Form

Client: _____ Project: _____ Job: _____

1. What deliverables does the client expect for this job? (Examples include letter, printed report, slide presentation, database file, template, spreadsheet.)

2. Which additional resources, if any, do you need in finding information to complete the job? (Examples include Internet searches and documents on disk.)

3. What software do you need to complete this job?

4. What special software formatting features does the job call for?

STUDENT LOG

Name: _____ Date/Time Completed: _____

Document File Name(s): _____

Comments:

Client: _____ Athletic House Sports Center _____ Project: _____ p1j2 _____

Job #2

Files Needed
application.doc
logo.bmp

Frank McKenzie feels that the current AHSC membership application form needs revision to improve its appearance. The form should be one that prospective customers will notice and that will present a positive company image. Current practice is to distribute the form to potential clients who visit one of the fitness centers; applicants then complete it with a pen. Plans are to place the form on the company Web site in a couple of months, so Frank wants it designed in a way that will make this transition as easy as possible. On the phone last week, he and Ronald Powell decided on several improvements, which Ronald noted in the list that follows.

✔ Format the application form so that it will fit onto one page.

✔ Insert the company logo in the top-left corner. Place the company name immediately under the logo for an attractive appearance.

✔ Use WordArt to enter the company name, address, and telephone number. Center these elements, varying the size of the entry so that the company name is larger than the address.

✔ Center the form title ("Membership Application") below the phone number. Use shading and/or color to make it more attractive and distinctive.

✔ Use shading to emphasize the entire "Type of Membership" section. Add the following membership type to the form: Corporate Membership (10-person minimum), $600.

✔ Since many clients prefer to be contacted by e-mail, add a blank entry section below the blanks for telephone and fax numbers.

Client: _____ Athletic House Sports Center _____ Project: _____ p1j2 _____

AHSC Membership Application

MEMBERSHIP
APPLICATION

Athletic House Sports Center
2364 Park Terrace Avenue
Los Angeles, California 93721

(800) 555-5444   (323) 555-2222   Fax: (323) 555-2223

Please complete all information below for future AHSC correspondence.

First Name   M.I.   Last Name

Street Address

City   State/Province   Zip/Postal Code   Country

Area Code-Telephone Number   Area Code-Fax Number

☐ Members' addresses are sometimes provided to companies who offer fitness products and services. Members' phone numbers are *not* provided. If you prefer not to be included in these lists, check the box on the left.

☐ **New Member**   ☐ **Renewing Member**
Membership is effective for one year from the date of the membership contract. Dues are nonrefundable.

Type of Membership
Check one type of membership from the following options (subtract $100 if renewing member):

☐	Single Adult Membership (1)	$ 885
☐	Couple Membership (2)	$1500 _____

One Additional Name

☐   Family Membership (4-person maximum) $2085 _____
_____
_____

Up to Three Additional Names

☐   Student Membership (valid ID required) $ 785 _____

ID Number if Applicable

☐   Senior Citizen Membership (55 years or older) $ 785 _____

Birth Date

Method of Payment
☐ Check (made payable to AHSC)
☐ Visa   ☐ MasterCard   ☐ American Express   ☐ Discover
Card Number: _____   Expiration Date: _____

Print name as it appears on card: _____
Signature: _____   Date: _____

Client: _____ Project: _____ Job: _____

1. What deliverables does the client expect for this job? (Examples include letter, printed report, slide presentation, database file, template, spreadsheet.)

2. Which additional resources, if any, do you need in finding information to complete the job? (Examples include Internet searches and documents on disk.)

3. What software do you need to complete this job?

4. What special software formatting features does the job call for?

STUDENT LOG

Name: _____ Date/Time Completed: _____

Document File Name(s): _____

Comments:

Client: **Athletic House Sports Center**   Project: **p1j3**

Job #3

Files Needed
roster.xls

Ronald Powell received the following e-mail message from Frank McKenzie. A customized form letter must be written and mailed to each person on the roster attachment. Frank prefers that the letter be three paragraphs long.

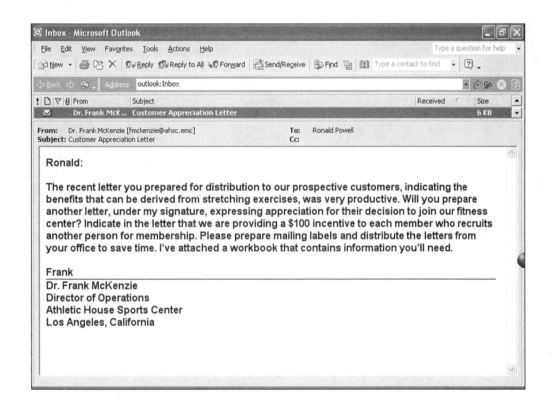

Inbox - Microsoft Outlook

File Edit View Favorites Tools Actions Help

From: Dr. Frank McKenzie [fmckenzie@ahsc.emc]   **To:** Ronald Powell
Subject: Customer Appreciation Letter   **Cc:**

Ronald:

The recent letter you prepared for distribution to our prospective customers, indicating the benefits that can be derived from stretching exercises, was very productive. Will you prepare another letter, under my signature, expressing appreciation for their decision to join our fitness center? Indicate in the letter that we are providing a $100 incentive to each member who recruits another person for membership. Please prepare mailing labels and distribute the letters from your office to save time. I've attached a workbook that contains information you'll need.

Frank
Dr. Frank McKenzie
Director of Operations
Athletic House Sports Center
Los Angeles, California

Business Technology Consultants

Client: _____ Project: _____ Job: _____

1. What deliverables does the client expect for this job? (Examples include letter, printed report, slide presentation, database file, template, spreadsheet.)

2. Which additional resources, if any, do you need in finding information to complete the job? (Examples include Internet searches and documents on disk.)

3. What software do you need to complete this job?

4. What special software formatting features does the job call for?

STUDENT LOG

Name: _____ Date/Time Completed: _____

Document File Name(s): _____

Comments:

Client: **Athletic House Sports Center**   Project: **p2j1**

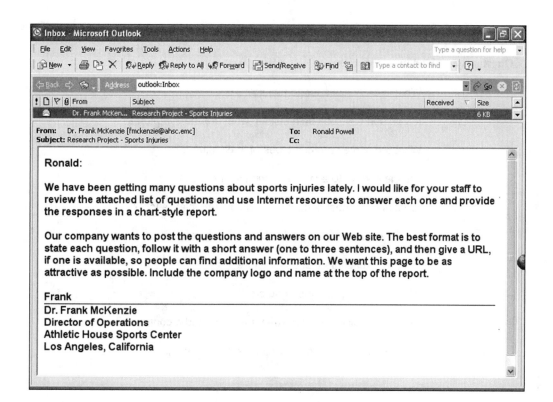

Job #1

Files Needed
logo.bmp

Ronald Powell and Frank McKenzie met for lunch to look at the list of questions and discuss the Web chart. Frank asked that each question be shown in a color to draw attention to it and to enhance readability (he suggested blue). Ronald thinks the material will best be presented in a three-column table with the question in the first column, the response in the second, and the URL in the third. Use AutoFormat to make the table more attractive. Save the document in Word and also as a Web page so that it can be viewed in a Web format to see how it will function on the AHSC Web site. Format designs can be changed, if needed, until a design is developed that will be attractive on the Web. The questions are on the next page.

Client: _____ Athletic House Sports Center _____ Project: _____ p2j1 _____

Questions provided by AHSC clients:

1. What is an Achilles tendon injury?

2. If a person develops shin splints, what are the symptoms?

3. What are some common types of knee injuries?

4. Are there ways to avoid hamstring injuries?

5. What are the most common symptoms of athlete's foot?

6. How should a sprained ankle be medically treated?

7. What is a metatarsal stress fracture?

8. What are the symptoms of bursitis?

9. What is the difference between a fracture and a contusion?

10. What are some common symptoms of neuroma pain?

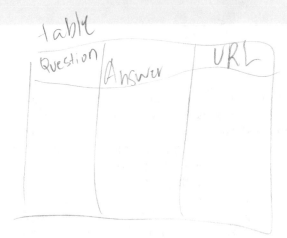

Job Planning Form

Client: _____ Project: _____ Job: _____

1. What deliverables does the client expect for this job? (Examples include letter, printed report, slide presentation, database file, template, spreadsheet.)

2. Which additional resources, if any, do you need in finding information to complete the job? (Examples include Internet searches and documents on disk.)

3. What software do you need to complete this job?

4. What special software formatting features does the job call for?

STUDENT LOG

Name: _____ Date/Time Completed: _____

Document File Name(s): _____

Comments:

Client: **Athletic House Sports Center**   Project: **p3j1**

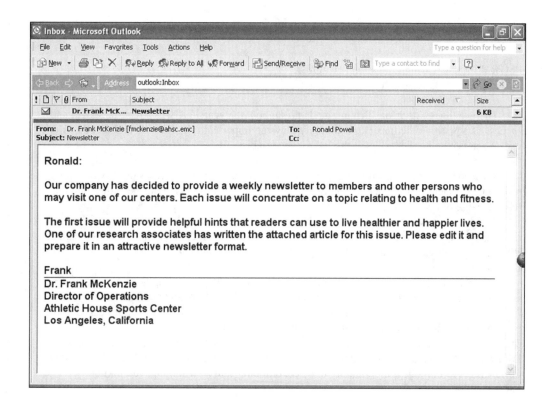

Job #1

Files Needed
news.doc
dues.xls

When Ronald Powell called Frank McKenzie to talk about the layout, they agreed on a two-column format. Frank wants the newsletter to be exactly two pages long, and said it will be acceptable to adjust font, spacing, and graphic sizes as needed to make the material fit evenly. If needed, text can also be added or deleted in order to meet the two-page requirement. Frank prefers to use endnotes as a way to indicate citations in the article. He indicated points in the text where the endnote notations should be inserted. The article Frank sent begins on the next page.

Physical Fitness: Living Longer and Healthier
By Nanalee Roark, Research Associate

There are many decisions that are made throughout the years that will affect the length and success of a person's lifetime. While heredity plays an important role, lifestyle and diet do as well. Each person has control over the latter two variables.

Don't Smoke

Tobacco increases the heart rate and raises blood pressure, which increases the risk of angina, heart attacks, aneurysms, hypertension, blood clots, and cancer. Smoking has been declared the leading cause of death in the United States.

A person who wants to quit smoking should set a specific date, get support from friends, use medication such as nicotine gum if needed, and avoid being around other smokers. Good eating habits and proper exercise can also help a person break a smoking habit.

Do Exercise

Aerobic activities provide for a stronger heart and lungs. Brisk walking, jogging, and cycling are good activities to reduce the risk of heart disease. The Health Institute of America predicts that even a moderate amount of exercise on a regular basis can reduce the threat of heart disease by 50 percent. **<Insert the first endnote reference notation>**

Many health advocates recommend vigorous exercise four times a week with each activity lasting at least 30 minutes. Some activities that are categorized as vigorous include aerobic walking or dancing, bicycling, jogging, running in place, climbing stairs, swimming, and hiking.

Do Stay Slim

Extra pounds can add to the risk of heart disease and stroke. Diabetes and cancer are more likely to occur in people who are overweight.

Lifestyle changes may be required in order to lose weight. A good program should include proper diet and exercise programs.

Do Avoid Stress

People who are stressed or angry much of the time are more likely to have heart disease or stroke. Positive relationships with others will reduce stress and provide for a healthier lifestyle.

A regular physical fitness program along with a positive attitude and balanced diet will help to avoid stress. Relaxing exercises such as yoga and meditation may also help.

Do Control Cholesterol

High cholesterol tends to clog the arteries and reduce blood circulation in the body. Cholesterol levels usually become a problem after the age of 40. HDL has been called the good cholesterol and should be maintained in the 40 to 50 range if possible. LDL has been called the bad cholesterol and should be maintained below 130.

Diet and exercise are the only sure ways to control cholesterol without medication, which is required in certain cases. Some medications have long-term side effects, so proper diet and exercise are highly recommended as a way to avoid or reduce high cholesterol levels.

Client: **Athletic House Sports Center**   Project: **p3j1**

Do Watch Blood Pressure

High blood pressure has been called the "silent killer" because many people do not know that they have it. There are often few, if any, symptoms to indicate this condition. High blood pressure makes it more difficult for the heart to pump blood to vital organs of the body; it can also contribute to stroke and kidney disease.

Excess alcohol, excess salt, and a fatty diet can contribute to high blood pressure, as can birth control pills (for women). Fish, vegetables, fruits, potassium, magnesium, and fiber in foods can help to lower the blood pressure. In addition, a good physical fitness program has been shown to lower blood pressure.

Do Avoid Depression

Anger and depression are contributors to bad health. Depression is more common than many people realize because most people who experience it do not tell their friends and family. People who are angry or depressed tend to have more health problems than other people.

Depression often does not go away without medication. However, in some instances an upbeat attitude that can be fostered by a good exercise program can make a positive difference in how a depressed person feels.

Do Join a Physical Fitness Program

Physical fitness and exercise are not the cure for all health problems. Notice, however, how many concerns cited in this article can be prevented or alleviated by a sound physical fitness and exercise program which, along with proper diet, can increase the chances for maintaining a healthy lifestyle. **<Insert the second endnote reference notation here.>** A fitness program is not as expensive as many people may imagine it to be. Rates for a two-year program at AHSC are shown below. **<Insert dues workbook information here.>**

Do Visit a Physician

A physician is often the only person who can easily and quickly diagnose many of the problems associated with health risk indicators such as high blood pressure and high cholesterol. The personal trainers employed at any of the Athletic House Sports Center locations, all of whom are fully certified, are qualified to cooperate as team members with you and your physician to develop a fitness program that is customized for specific health needs.

<Format the Endnotes appropriately>

References cited in the article:

Health Institute of America, "Exercise and Your Health: A Guide to Physical Fitness," pamphlet no. 47-2753.

Health Institute of America, "Living a Longer, Healthier Lifestyle with Diet and Exercise," pamphlet no. 52-3742.

Job Planning Form

• • • **Job Planning Form** • • •

Client: _____ Project: _____ Job: _____

1. What deliverables does the client expect for this job? (Examples include letter, printed report, slide presentation, database file, template, spreadsheet.)

2. Which additional resources, if any, do you need in finding information to complete the job? (Examples include Internet searches and documents on disk.)

3. What software do you need to complete this job?

4. What special software formatting features does the job call for?

STUDENT LOG

Name: _____ Date/Time Completed: _____

Document File Name(s): _____

Comments:

Client: _____ Athletic House Sports Center _____ Project: _____ p4j1 _____

Job #1

Files Needed
ahsc.mdb

AHSC is upgrading its membership database. Frank McKenzie sent Ronald Powell a sample database table (below) for review and testing. The table will be used to locate members and related information such as phone numbers. In a follow-up meeting, he gave Ronald a list of four additional members to add to the database. In addition, he requested several corrections to the table:

- Change the name of the field mem_type to type to reduce the column width.
- Change the phone number for Jane Weid to 209/555-2187.
- Change the name Ellie Harrell to Ellie Mercer.
- Print a listing of all members in the revised table in ascending alphabetical order by last name and by first name.

    The company wants all fields of this table to fit onto one page, so landscape print mode may be necessary.

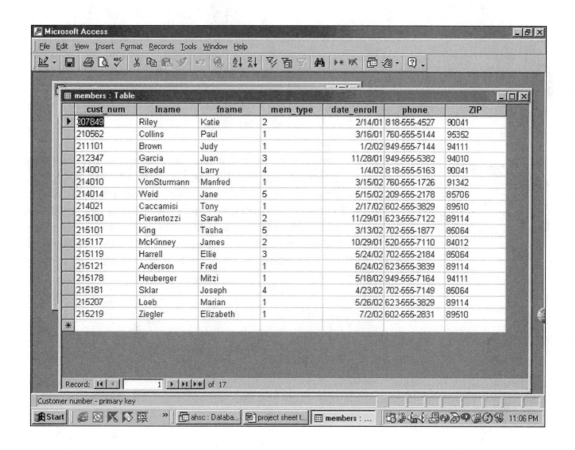

cust_num	lname	fname	mem_type	date_enroll	phone	ZIP
207849	Riley	Katie	2	2/14/01	818-555-4527	90041
210562	Collins	Paul	1	3/16/01	760-555-5144	95352
211101	Brown	Judy	1	1/2/02	949-555-7144	94111
212347	Garcia	Juan	3	11/28/01	949-555-5382	94010
214001	Ekedal	Larry	4	1/4/02	818-555-5163	90041
214010	VonSturmann	Manfred	1	3/15/02	760-555-1726	91342
214014	Weid	Jane	5	5/15/02	209-555-2178	85706
214021	Caccamisi	Tony	1	2/17/02	602-555-3829	89510
215100	Pierantozzi	Sarah	2	11/29/01	623-555-7122	89114
215101	King	Tasha	5	3/13/02	702-555-1877	85064
215117	McKinney	James	2	10/29/01	520-555-7110	84012
215119	Harrell	Ellie	3	5/24/02	702-555-2184	85064
215121	Anderson	Fred	1	6/24/02	623-555-3839	89114
215178	Heuberger	Mitzi	1	5/18/02	949-555-7164	94111
215181	Sklar	Joseph	4	4/23/02	702-555-7149	85064
215207	Loeb	Marian	1	5/26/02	623-555-3829	89114
215219	Ziegler	Elizabeth	1	7/2/02	602-555-2831	89510

Record: 1 of 17

Customer number - primary key

Client: **Athletic House Sports Center**   Project: **p4j1**

Additional Members for Database

215109	214009
Bottoms	Pearson
Ann	Joyce
2	1
7/24/2002	6/25/2002
760/555-2843	949/555-2674
91342	94111

210845	215210
Chou	DuBose
Dong	Chris
3	1
5/25/2002	6/10/2002
623/555-4387	949/555-7219
89114	94010

Job #1

**(continued)
Files Needed**
ahsc.mdb

At the meeting, Frank told Ronald that the following queries are typical of the ones that will be used with this database table. He asked Ronald to run the queries and show him how the results will appear in a report format, such as a corporate one, for each query. He likes all reports to be sorted on the last name by first name fields, but prefers that the first name be printed to the left of the last name in all reports that include the names of members.

Query Requests

1. Listing of the names of members sorted in ascending alphabetical order along with members' phone numbers
2. Listing of the names and zip codes of members sorted by zip code
3. Listing of the names and zip codes of members who reside in the following zip code: 94111
4. Listing of the names of members and type of membership for members who reside in the 94111 zip code area and have a single adult membership (membership type 1)
5. Listing of the names and phone numbers of members who enrolled prior to January 1, 2002
6. Listing of the names and phone numbers of members who reside in the 89114 zip code area or have a phone number with a 949 as the area code.
7. Listing of the customer numbers, names, and phone numbers of all members with a customer number that is between 214000 and 215120
8. Listing of customer names and membership types for all members with membership types 1 or 2

Job Planning Form

● ● ● **Job Planning Form** ● ● ●

Client: _____ Project:_____ Job: _____

1. What deliverables does the client expect for this job? (Examples include letter, printed report, slide presentation, database file, template, spreadsheet.)

2. Which additional resources, if any, do you need in finding information to complete the job? (Examples include Internet searches and documents on disk.)

3. What software do you need to complete this job?

4. What special software formatting features does the job call for?

STUDENT LOG

Name: _____ Date/Time Completed: _____

Document File Name(s): _____

Comments:

Client: **Athletic House Sports Center**   Project: **p4j2**

Job #2

Files Needed
receipt.xls
application.doc

In conjunction with the membership database upgrade, AHSC wants a workbook that can be used to print receipts. That firm's staff has designed a fairly attractive workbook (below). Frank McKenzie wants BTC to add some features that will make it more functional. He would like the data entry clerks to be able to enter the membership type number and have the software look up the membership description and amount due. An appropriate table should be added to support this function. He also requested that the current date be entered automatically. Ronald Powell told Frank he would consult with BTC's office productivity specialist, Joe Brown, regarding how best to develop the table.

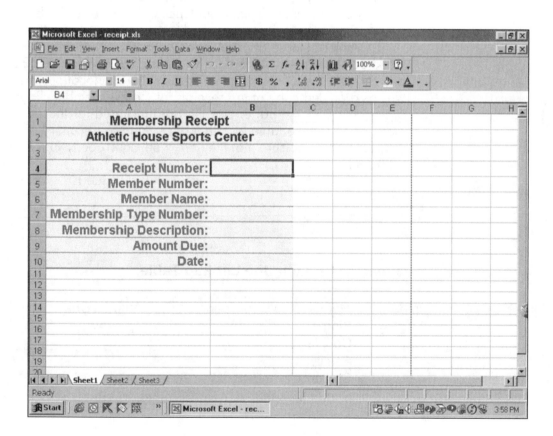

Client: _____ Athletic House Sports Center _____ Project: _____ p4j2 _____

Job #2

(continued)
Files Needed
receipt.xls
application.doc

Joe Brown told Ronald that a lookup table will be needed to permit the software to look up the description and amount due entries based on the membership type value. Joe suggested that the print macro be named "P" to make it easy to remember. The macro should also include instructions to (a) clear the values that have been entered and then (b) return the pointer to the location where the receipt number can be entered for the next person. The macro should begin in cell J3. The Sheet 1 tab should be named "Receipt" in case additional sheets are added at a later date.

Values to be used for creating (adding) the lookup table are shown below. Retrieve the membership application form (Project 1, Job 2) that was created earlier to get the amount due values. Format the amount due values as currency with two places to the right of the decimal point. Place the lookup table values, including the column headings, in cells C15 to E20. Joe suggested that the Excel Help function be reviewed to be sure that the values are entered in the required sequence.

Athletic House Sports Center wants a copy of the workbook template (with lookup formulas displayed for cells B8 and B9) and the lookup table values to show cell locations, as well as a printed copy of test receipts for the five members listed at the bottom of the page. Use the data included for those members to test the table lookup feature, macro execution, and date function to be sure that they are working properly in the workbook.

Values for Creating the Lookup Table

Membership Type Number	Membership Description	Amount Due
1	Single	
2	Couple	
3	Family	
4	Student	
5	Senior Citizen	

Client: _____ Athletic House Sports Center _____ Project: _____ p4j2 _____

Test Data

Receipt Number	Member Number	Member Name	Membership Type No.
10001	212345	Willard Paylak	2
10002	212346	Arlene Yarbro	5
10003	212347	Juan Garcia	3
10004	212348	Donna Toole	1
10005	212349	Gwen Herndon	4

Business Technology Consultants

Client: _____ Project:_____ Job: _____

1. What deliverables does the client expect for this job? (Examples include letter, printed report, slide presentation, database file, template, spreadsheet.)

2. Which additional resources, if any, do you need in finding information to complete the job? (Examples include Internet searches and documents on disk.)

3. What software do you need to complete this job?

4. What special software formatting features does the job call for?

STUDENT LOG

Name: _____ Date/Time Completed: _____

Document File Name(s): _____

Comments:

Business Technology Consultants
Project and Job Information

Client: **Athletic House Sports Center**   Project: **p5j1**

Job #1

Files Needed
None

Ronald Powell uses the Microsoft Outlook Calendar feature to maintain his calendar on a daily basis so that appointments, deadlines, and events will not be missed. First thing Monday morning he needs a printed copy of the week's calendar of events. Below is an example of Ronald's calendar. Select an Outlook calendar format and use the notes that Ronald provided (see the next page) to make the necessary entries.

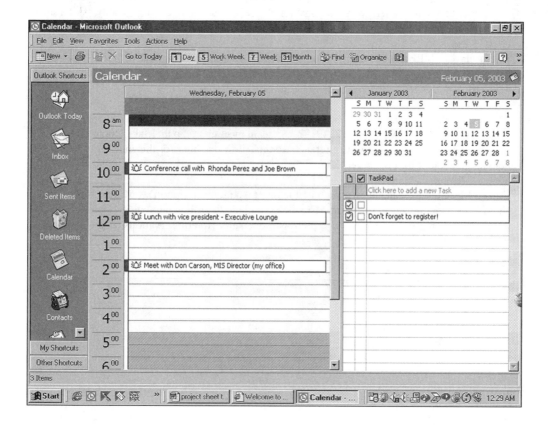

Client: _____ Athletic House Sports Center _____ Project: _____ p5j1 _____

Calendar Notes: RP

Monday: Meet with Don Carson, MIS director, in his office (Room 323) at 9 a.m. Add a note that this meeting should last for about one hour. Lunch meeting at noon with the Rotary Club. Add a note to include the following items: The location will be the Food Court Restaurant. This meeting should last for about two hours. Bruce Gresham from the Chamber of Commerce is the luncheon speaker.

Tuesday: Conference call with Frank McKenzie at 10 a.m. Add a note that Frank will call me to arrange the call and that his company's vice president, Marilyn Kelley, will also take part in the conference call. This conference should last for about 30 minutes. She will probably ask for an update on the newsletter project that we are doing for the AHSC.

Wednesday: Call Robert Herring as soon as possible to see if he can meet with me sometime today. His extension is 2743. Make a note that Robert has been on a one-week vacation and will return to work this morning.

Thursday: Call Don Carson at 9 a.m. Make a note that his opinion about the AHSC database project is needed. His extension is 2849. Project team meeting at 2 p.m. Make a note that the meeting will be in the Executive Conference Room. Allow one hour for this meeting. Make a note that the folder for Project A2725 may be needed at the meeting.

Friday: Block out the calendar for the day. I leave at 9 a.m. for a trip to Des Moines, Iowa, with Vicki Robertson, president of Interior Creations. Include the following details: Delta Flight #348A34, arriving in Des Moines at 1 p.m. with one stop. Hotel reservations (confirmation #BC27342) at the Clark Ridge Inn.

Client: _____ Project: _____ Job: _____

1. What deliverables does the client expect for this job? (Examples include letter, printed report, slide presentation, database file, template, spreadsheet.)

2. Which additional resources, if any, do you need in finding information to complete the job? (Examples include Internet searches and documents on disk.)

3. What software do you need to complete this job?

4. What special software formatting features does the job call for?

STUDENT LOG

Name: _____ Date/Time Completed: _____

Document File Name(s): _____

Comments:

Client: _____ Athletic House Sports Center _____ Project: _____ p6j1 _____

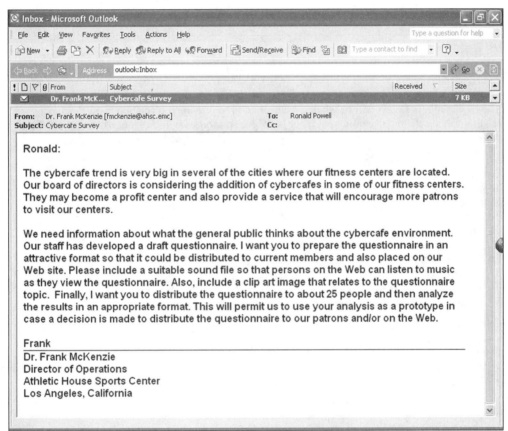

Publisher

Job #1

NOTES

Files Needed
cybercafe.doc
cyber.mid
cyber.wmf

Accompanying Frank McKenzie's e-mail was the questionnaire file along with a sound file and a clip art image. In a follow-up conversation, he told Ronald Powell that BTC has the discretion to choose a different image and audio clip. The sound file can be included to the left of the heading, the clip art image to the right. At the beginning of the questionnaire, include a one-sentence statement to define cybercafe terminology, citing the URL that was the source of the definition. For question 1, Frank suggested that a check box be included to the left of each of the listed choices. For question 7, include a text box to permit people to write comments. Frank indicated that students and/or employees could be included in the 25-person sample. He wants results for each of the first six items to be shown graphically. He also wants the complete results presented in a short report that includes text along with the graphics. The questionnaire draft begins on the next page.

make up
excel
graph

Client: _____ Athletic House Sports Center _____ Project: _____ p6j1 _____

Questionnaire Draft

Cybercafe Survey

The results of this survey will be tabulated and charted to provide information about opinions relating to the cybercafe environment. Your individual responses will be grouped for analysis with those of others who complete the survey, so confidentiality will be maintained.

1. Why would you consider visiting a cybercafe? (Check all that apply.)

To connect to a computer while traveling and/or on vacation
To play network games
To work on a computer and eat at the same time
To socialize with friends
To e-mail someone while away from home
To participate in a Net meeting or videoconference
To create a Web page
To participate in real-time chats
To make online purchases

2. During the past year, how many times have you visited a cybercafe?

One time or less
2–5 times
6–9 times
10 times or more

3. Do you think that cybercafes will be more popular in five years than they are today?

Yes
No
Not sure

4. Do you think that a cybercafe would be a good addition to a fitness center?

Yes
No
Not sure

5. Please rank the following factors that might influence your decision to join a fitness club that has a cybercafe. Use 1 as the highest ranking.

Convenience
Price
Quality
Services

6. Do you think that cybercafes are a passing fad?

Yes
No
Not sure

7. Please provide any additional comments that you would like to make regarding cybercafes.

Job Planning Form

Client: _____ Project: _____ Job: _____

1. What deliverables does the client expect for this job? (Examples include letter, printed report, slide presentation, database file, template, spreadsheet.)

2. Which additional resources, if any, do you need in finding information to complete the job? (Examples include Internet searches and documents on disk.)

3. What software do you need to complete this job?

4. What special software formatting features does the job call for?

STUDENT LOG

Name: _____ Date/Time Completed: _____

Document File Name(s): _____

Comments:

Client: **Athletic House Sports Center**   Project: **p7j1**

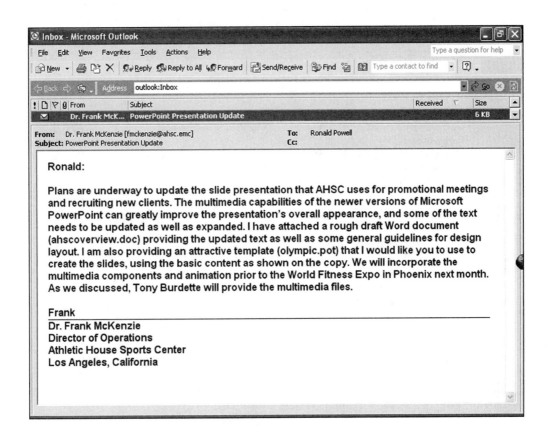

Job #1

Files Needed
olympic.pot
ahscoverview.doc
ahsclogoround.gif

The basic text content and instructions for the new PowerPoint presentation begin on the next page. First, create the 13 initial slides. Apply the template design called olympic.pot for the presentation and format all text with appropriate colors, fonts, and sizes to improve the appearance of the presentation and correspond to the template color scheme. Then follow the steps for adding WordArt, action buttons, and graphic images.

Client: _____ Athletic House Sports Center _____ Project: _____ p7j1 _____

Updated Text and Design Guidelines

CREATING THE SLIDES

1. Use **ATHLETIC HOUSE SPORTS CENTER** for the title and www.ahsc.emc for the subtitle.

    | SLIDE 1 |

2. Use **AHSC MAKES IT EASY FOR YOU TO GET AND STAY FIT** for the title and **DO SOMETHING FOR YOURSELF TODAY!** for the subtitle.

    | SLIDE 2 |

3. Use **FIT FOR LIFE . . . FUNDAMENTALS** for the title and enter the bulleted items as shown below:

    | SLIDE 3 |

•**Food Intake . . . Eat smart, not less.**
•**Cardiorespiratory Training . . . Give your heart a regular beat.**
•**Food Supplementation . . . The small stuff can make a big difference.**
•**Resistance Training . . . Redefine yourself!**
•**Professional Assistance . . . Get with the program.**

4. Enter the title and bulleted items shown below:

FITNESS CLASSES

| SLIDE 4 |

•**Step Aerobics – high-intensity, low-impact workout using an adjustable bench**
•**Group Cycle – basic, athletic, and rhythmic drills on indoor cycles**
•**Low Impact – aerobics with little or no bouncing, jumping, or hopping**
•**Step and Sculpt – high-intensity, low-impact workout using an adjustable bench, with muscle conditioning**
•**Hi/Low – rhythmic cardiovascular workout**
•**Turbo Kick – kickboxing for cardiovascular workout**

5. Enter the title and bulleted items shown below:

FIT FOR LIFE KIDS

| SLIDE 5 |

•**Hip-Hop**
•**Karate**
•**Tumbling**
•**Swimming**
•**Cycling**
•**Gymnastics**

6. Enter the title and bulleted list shown below:

MEASURING FITNESS

| SLIDE 6 |

Client: _____ Athletic House Sports Center _____ Project: _____ p7j1 _____

•**Body Mass Index (BMI)** –
Calculate average weight in relation to height.
•**Resting Metabolic Rate (RMR)** –
Calculate number of calories burned when inactive.
•**Burn Calculator (BC)** –
Calculate number of calories burned when active.
•**Daily Caloric Intake (DCI) Needs** –
Calculate number of calories needed to maintain desired weight.

7.   Enter the title and bulleted list shown below:

FITNESS ACTIVITY LEVELS   SLIDE 7

•**Very Light – sitting, studying, talking, little walking**
•**Light – keying, teaching, some walking**
•**Moderate – walking, jogging, gardening**
•**Heavy – digging, climbing**
•**Exceptionally Heavy – weight training, aerobic dance**
•**Sports – vigorous sports competition**
•**All-Out Training – extremely high-intensity weight training**
•**Extended Maximum Effort – extremely high intensity and high duration**

8.   Enter the title and bulleted list shown below:

FLEXIBLE FITNESS TRAINING BENEFITS   SLIDE 8

•**Decreased Risk of Injury**
•**Improved Posture**
•**Increased Blood Supply**
•**Increased Neuromuscular Coordination**
•**Relaxed Mind and Body**

9.   Enter the title and bulleted list shown below:

CERTIFIED PERSONAL TRAINERS   SLIDE 9

•**Degrees in Exercise Science**
•**Professional Expertise**
•**Diagnostics and Customized Training**
•**Long-Term Scheduling**
•**Personalized Video Workout Programs**
•**Motivation and Encouragement**

Client: **Athletic House Sports Center**   Project: **p7j1**

---

10. Enter the title and bulleted list shown below:

CERTIFYING AGENCIES

SLIDE 10

•**AFPA –**
American Fitness Professionals and Associates
•**CSCS –**
Certified Strength and Conditioning Specialists
•**NAFC –**
National Association for Fitness Certification
•**NASM –**
National Academy of Sports Medicine
•**NESTA –**
National Endurance Sports Training Association

11. Enter the title and bulleted list shown below:

PRODUCTS AND EQUIPMENT

SLIDE 11

•**Fitness/Exercise Equipment**
•**Nutritional Supplements**
•**Fitness Wear/Apparel**
•**Fitness Videos**
•**Fitness Books/Audiotapes**

12. Use **AHSC MEMBERSHIPS** for the title and use a table layout, entering the following information in the table cells:

SLIDE 12

Type	Fee	Restrictions
Single Adult	$885.00	1
Couple	$1,500.00	2
Family	$2,085.00	Maximum 4
Student	$785.00	ID Required
Senior Citizen	$785.00	Age 55 or More
Corporate	$600.00	Minimum 10

13. Use **ATHLETIC HOUSE SPORTS CENTER** for the title and include the following additional information:

2364 Park Terrace Avenue
Los Angeles, California 93721

SLIDE 13

Client: _____ Athletic House Sports Center _____ Project: _____ p7j1 _____

Dr. Frank McKenzie
Director of Operations

ADDING 3D WORDART TO SLIDES

1. On Slide 1, change the title to appear as WordArt and use the 3D button on the Drawing toolbar to create a title similar to the one shown below.

2. Use the 3D Settings toolbar to adjust the 3D lighting, depth, and color.
3. Use these same tools to create 3D WordArt titles on Slides 5, 9, 11, and 13 as shown.

Client: _____ Athletic House Sports Center _____ Project: _____ p7j1 _____

ADDING MULTIMEDIA ACTION BUTTONS TO SLIDES

1. Beginning with Slide 1, create action buttons for easily moving from slide to slide. This will make the slide presentation interactive and user-friendly.
2. On the pull-down menu, select Slide Show and Action Buttons.
3. Use the Forward or Next button and use the mouse to draw the button in an appropriate location on the slide.

4. Use the Hyperlink to: Next Slide option and Play Sound option. Select Slide Projector for the sound file.
5. Drag the small gold diamond to the right to give the button more depth.
6. Use the Fill Color and Line Color buttons to improve the appearance of the Next button.
7. Copy the Next button and paste it on all remaining slides except the last one.
8. Beginning with Slide 2, select Slide Show and Action Buttons again.
9. Select the Back or Previous button and use the mouse to draw the button in an appropriate location on the slide.
10. Select the Hyperlink to: Previous Slide option and play the Slide Projector sound file.
11. Drag the small gold diamond to the right to give the button more depth.
12. Use the Fill Color and Line Color buttons to improve the appearance of the Previous button.
13. Copy and paste the Previous button on Slides 3–13.
14. On Slide 13, add a Home action button with the Slide Projector sound that links to the first slide since it is the final slide in the presentation.

ADDING 3D GRAPHIC IMAGES

1. Beginning with Slide 1, add the company logo (ahsclogoround.gif) at least once to each slide in the presentation along with the corresponding 3D WordArt as shown below:

2. Add additional clip art images to improve the general appearance of the basic presentation.
3. Add appropriate Transition and Build Effects using the Sorter View of the presentation.

· · · Job Planning Form · · ·

Client: _____ Project: _____ Job: _____

1. What deliverables does the client expect for this job? (Examples include letter, printed report, slide presentation, database file, template, spreadsheet.)

2. Which additional resources, if any, do you need in finding information to complete the job? (Examples include Internet searches and documents on disk.)

3. What software do you need to complete this job?

4. What special software formatting features does the job call for?

STUDENT LOG

Name: _____ Date/Time Completed: _____

Document File Name(s): _____

Comments:

Job Planning Form   Integrated Computer Projects   113

Client: _____Athletic House Sports Center_____ Project: _____p7j2_____

Job #2

Files Needed
(see below)

Tony Burdette of BTC provided several recommendations to BTC for converting the basic PowerPoint presentation to a multimedia presentation Frank can use at the World Fitness Expo. Tony prepared several audio and video files as well as graphic images to simplify the task of making these multimedia improvements. His instructions to Ronald Powell begin on the next page.

AUDIO FILES NEEDED

Slide	File
1	ahsconline.mp3
2	ahscaudiomotto.mp3
3	ahscfundamentals.mp3
4	ahscclasses.mp3
5	ahsckids.mp3
6	ahscmeasures.mp3
7	ahscactivitylevels.mp3
8	flexiblebenefits.mp3
9	personaltrainers.mp3
10	certagencies.mp3
11	productsequip.mp3
12	memberships.mp3
13	ahscaddress.mp3
	ahscclosing.mp3

VIDEO FILES NEEDED

Slide	File
2	electro.avi
5	musicvideo3.avi

GRAPHIC IMAGES NEEDED

Slide	File
1	olympicathletes.jpg
2	ahsclogoround.gif
3	athleticwoman.jpg
4	athleticwoman2.jpg
5	childswimmer.jpg
	swimmingpool.jpg
6	calculatoranimated.gif
	lifteranimated.gif
7	crunches.gif
	liftweights2.gif
	runneranimated.gif

Client: _____ Athletic House Sports Center _____ Project: _____ p7j2 _____

INSERTING AUDIO FILES

1. Use the Insert, Movies and Sounds, and Sound from File options to add each audio file to the correct slide. Each sound should play automatically when the slide appears on the screen. Notice that the final slide has two audio files associated with it.
2. Place the small audio icon in an appropriate location on each slide to provide the replay option for the viewer without obstructing the view of other elements on the slide.

INSERTING VIDEO FILES

1. Insert a video/movie in the center of Slide 2 using Insert, Movies and Sounds, Movie from File options to add the movie. Each movie should play automatically at the appropriate time as the elements of the slide appear on the screen.
2. On Slide 5, insert the music video to play automatically.

INSERTING A TEXT BOX CONTROL FIELD

1. Use View, Toolbars, Control Toolbox to select a Text Box control field to add to Slide 1.
2. Draw the box large enough to allow entry of an e-mail address by the viewer.
3. Place the control Text Box near the bottom of the slide.
4. Use the standard Text Box tool on the Drawing toolbar to add the following message above the box: **ENTER YOUR E-MAIL ADDRESS:**

ADDING ENHANCED GRAPHIC IMAGES

1. On Slide 1, insert and place the graphic image on the right side of the slide to balance the appearance of the opening slide. Move and resize the additional elements on the slide to appear in the center of the slide.
2. On Slide 2, insert the graphic image on each side of the video element.
3. Insert and position the images for Slides 3 and 4.
4. Insert and position the images for Slide 5. Use the swimming pool image as a background for the names of the classes.
5. Insert and position the images for Slide 6.
6. Insert and position the images for Slide 7.
7. Add any additional images to improve the appearance of Slides 8–11.
8. On Slide 12, add color enhancements to the table with fill colors and gridlines.

REHEARSING AND SETTING PLAY TIMINGS

1. Remove the Action Buttons from all of the slides, and use the Sorter View to rehearse timings and add them to the slides. Be sure to allow time for the viewer to read all of the text content, listen to the audio, and view each video as the show plays.

Client: _____ Athletic House Sports Center _____ Project: _____ p7j2 _____

2. Insert a new, blank Slide 14 to end the show before it loops.
3. Use Slide Show, Set Up Show, and select **Browsed at a kiosk (full screen)** from the available options. This option will automatically set the show to loop continuously until Esc is pressed.

Job Planning Form

• • • **Job Planning Form** • • •

Client: _____ Project: _____ Job: _____

1. What deliverables does the client expect for this job? (Examples include letter, printed report, slide presentation, database file, template, spreadsheet.)

2. Which additional resources, if any, do you need in finding information to complete the job? (Examples include Internet searches and documents on disk.)

3. What software do you need to complete this job?

4. What special software formatting features does the job call for?

STUDENT LOG

Name: _____ Date/Time Completed: _____

Document File Name(s): _____

Comments:

CLIENT 3 State Community College Association
Projects Overview

 **State Community College Association**

The State Community College Association (SCCA) is an organization that represents community colleges in the Midwest with more than 344,000 students who are pursuing degrees that will lead directly into a career or a transfer to a four-year college or university after graduation. Community colleges provide opportunities for their students to lead successful and productive lives after completion of programs at member institutions.

The association supports community colleges with services for students and faculty, promotional campaigns, fund-raising, and other activities that relate to functions needed by the institutions. Community colleges have a 100-year history of providing students the foundation to prepare for careers, advance in a livelihood, and expand civic and cultural competencies for living and working in a society that is dependent on technology and rapid communication.

SCCA's vision is for its member colleges to be the best possible providers of educational services in the United States. Superior curriculum, professional faculty, outstanding administrators, and dedicated staff allow SCCA schools to deliver on the promise to prepare every student to live and work in a world that is increasingly affected by technological developments and world events. The mission statement indicates a commitment to provide students with educational and cultural experiences that will meet the needs of graduates, the community, and society.

Services Requested

SCCA relies heavily on Business Technology Consultants (BTC) to provide advice and support to both the organization and its member institutions. Typical services include obtaining information about career opportunities for graduates, preparing special educational projects, creating literature, evaluating survey results, reviewing enrollment trends, developing charts, meeting faculty educational needs, and helping with fund-raising campaigns. Ronald Powell's contact at SCCA is Ms. Elsie Dickerson, the director of support services. At present, Elsie has asked for Ronald's help on seven projects:

- **Project 1** (four jobs) requires researching, analyzing data, and creating literature for recruitment and fund-raising.
- **Project 2** (one job) calls on BTC to format a paper Elsie will present at a major professional meeting, following specific guidelines.
- **Project 3** (one job) involves designing the cover for the program for the SCCA annual conference.
- **Project 4** (one job) relates to creating a table and short report about a survey Elsie will present to the Chamber of Commerce.
- **Project 5** (one job) requires the creation of annotated charts on enrollment data.
- **Project 6** (four jobs) comprises tasks to support staff at member schools by preparing electronic grade-book templates for faculty members and developing a database, reports, and a chart of students and advisors.
- **Project 7** (one job) involves enhancing and updating the SCCA organizational chart.
- **Project 8** (one job) requires the creation of a database of students and advisors that allows faculty members to print various reports.

Client: State Community College Association   Project: p1j1

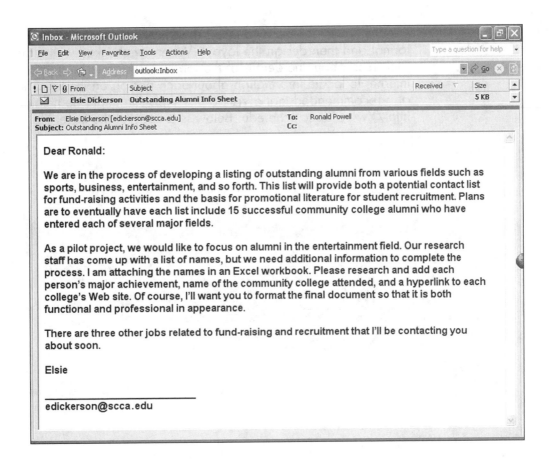

Business Technology Consultants
Project and Job Information

Client: _____State Community College Association_____ Project: _____p1j1_____

Job #1

Files Needed
alumni.xls

Ronald Powell's plan is to insert the Excel file into a Word format and then design the layout. When he checked with Elsie Dickerson about the details of the job, she suggested using the Internet to locate information about each person on the list. She also recommended that a visit to this Web site might be helpful: http://www.aacc.nche.edu. Below is a copy of the Excel file.

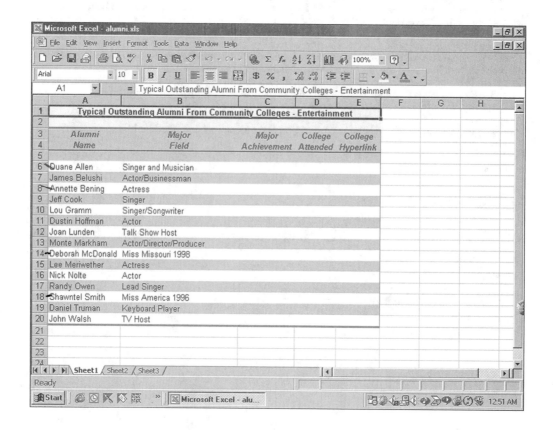

Job Planning Form

Client: _____ Project:_____ Job: _____

1. What deliverables does the client expect for this job? (Examples include letter, printed report, slide presentation, database file, template, spreadsheet.)

2. Which additional resources, if any, do you need in finding information to complete the job? (Examples include Internet searches and documents on disk.)

3. What software do you need to complete this job?

4. What special software formatting features does the job call for?

STUDENT LOG

Name: _____ Date/Time Completed: _____

Document File Name(s): _____

Comments:

Client: _____State Community College Association_____ Project: _____p1j2_____

```
Inbox - Microsoft Outlook

File  Edit  View  Favorites  Tools  Actions  Help              Type a question for help

Back          Address  outlook:Inbox                                      Go

! D ∇ 0 From           Subject                                      Received ∇   Size
  ✉      Elsie Dickerson   Letterhead and Fund Raising Letter                    5 KB

From:    Elsie Dickerson [edickerson@scca.edu]        To:    Ronald Powell
Subject: Letterhead and Fund Raising Letter           Cc:
```

Dear Ronald:

Our designers have developed an initial letterhead design. It looks fairly good, but I am still not totally satisfied with it. For one thing, I prefer not to have a box printed around the letterhead. Also, it looks a little plain. I would like to have a slight arch for our name—State Community College Association—to make it stand out more. In addition, I want the name to appear in a different font color—perhaps a dark blue. Otherwise, use your creativity to revise the letterhead so that it is professional and attractive. I'm having a copy of the initial design sent to you by overnight mail.

Along with the letterhead job, Dr. Sherra Witt, our director of development, wants you to design a mail-merge document that can be sent to financial supporters during our next fund-raising campaign. She drafted a letter for this purpose, which I will send to you. She also provided a workbook (attached) that has typical variables for the letter. I need you to code the letter and then use the revised letterhead to test the merge process using the variables in the workbook.

Please call if you have any questions. Thank you, Ronald.

Elsie _____
edickerson@scca.edu

Just letterhead

Client: _____ State Community College Association _____ Project: _____ p1j2 _____

Job #2

Files Needed
letterhead.doc

Below is the design Elsie Dickerson sent by overnight mail. Ronald Powell feels that Elsie's suggestion for changes to the appearance of the association's name is a good one. The logo may also need to be slightly resized. Ronald does not want to use WordArt to make the text less plain, but a different font may improve the appearance. Also, the table border should be changed to None. SCCA staff will retrieve the letterhead from a computer file each time that it is needed, and Elsie wants the current date to be automatically included with each retrieval.

State Community College Association

Midwest Regional Office
6139 Oakland Avenue
St. Louis, MO 63139

Phone: (314) 555-3728
Fax: (314) 555-3742
E-Mail: SCCA@scca.edu

Business Technology Consultants

• • • Job Planning Form • • •

Client: _____ Project: _____ Job: _____

1. What deliverables does the client expect for this job? (Examples include letter, printed report, slide presentation, database file, template, spreadsheet.)

2. Which additional resources, if any, do you need in finding information to complete the job? (Examples include Internet searches and documents on disk.)

3. What software do you need to complete this job?

4. What special software formatting features does the job call for?

STUDENT LOG

Name: _____ Date/Time Completed: _____

Document File Name(s): _____

Comments:

Client: **State Community College Association**   Project: _____ **p1j3** _____

Job #3

Files Needed
fund_letter.doc
donor_list.xls

Elsie Dickerson faxed a copy of the main document form-letter draft to Ronald Powell at BTC. She requested that a spelling and grammar check be performed on the letter and that any necessary corrections be made. Coding will be required in order to merge the variables from the workbook. The revised letterhead (Job 2) will also need to be added to the main document. Elsie asked that, prior to the merge process, the entries in the workbook be sorted in ascending order by zip code. She requested that a printed copy of the letter for the last person on the sorted list be provided to show results of the merge process. Following are the letter draft and donor list.

\<Letterhead plus the current date here\>

\<Address here\>

Dear **\<Title and last name here\>**:

Thank you for your generous support of our fund-raising campaigns during previous years. Your donation last year, **\<Last year's donation here\>**, provided support for our students and the SCCA academic programs.

Tuition and fees pay for only a small part of the cost required to provide an educational program that our students and benefactors deserve and want. Our most recent addition was the **\<The name of the addition here\>**. You are always welcome to come by and see the new facility during your next visit to our main campus in St. Louis.

Please use the enclosed envelop to send your contribution for this year. You can be sure that our students and faculty appreciate your support for our educational programs.

\<Closing lines here. The letter will be from Sherra Witt, Ph.D., Director of Development.\>

Business Technology Consultants
Project and Job Information

Client: _____State Community College Association_____ Project: _____p1j3_____

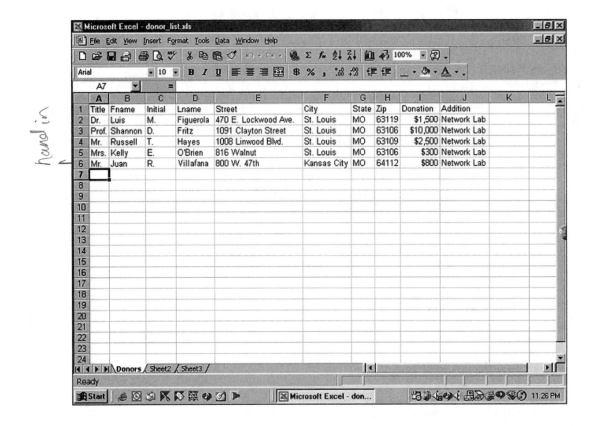

Job Planning Form

Client: _____ Project:_____ Job: _____

1. What deliverables does the client expect for this job? (Examples include letter, printed report, slide presentation, database file, template, spreadsheet.)

2. Which additional resources, if any, do you need in finding information to complete the job? (Examples include Internet searches and documents on disk.)

3. What software do you need to complete this job?

4. What special software formatting features does the job call for?

STUDENT LOG

Name: _____ Date/Time Completed: _____

Document File Name(s): _____

Comments:

Client: **State Community College Association** Project: **p1j4**

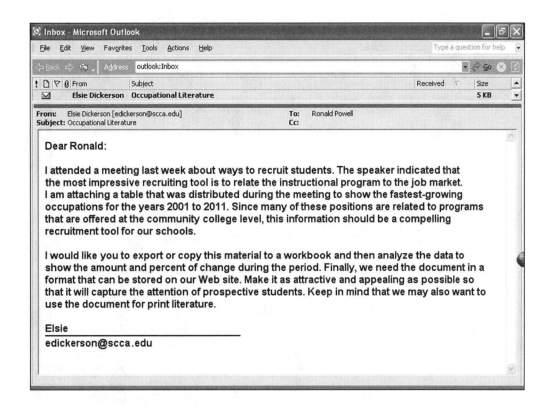

Job #4

Files Needed
jobs.doc

Elsie Dickerson followed her e-mail message with a phone call to Ronald Powell asking that a hyperlink be added to the table to indicate an Internet site where students can go for more information. She wants the hyperlink to be in the form of an appropriate clip art image with a notation to click on the image for additional information about careers. The image can be downloaded from an Internet site or a clip art gallery, as long as copyright laws are not violated.

Appropriate formulas are needed for the table. Since it will go on SCCA's Web site, Ronald asked Tony Burdette, BTC's graphic arts design specialist, to suggest ways to enhance the workbook document. Copies of the Word table and Tony's recommendations follow.

Client: State Community College Association   Project: p1j4

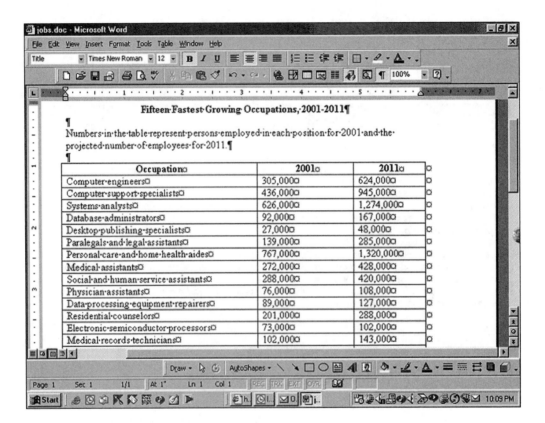

Client: **State Community College Association** Project: **p1j4**

Suggested Enhancements for Occupation Table

1. Name the worksheet tab with the following title: Jobs. Adjust column widths as needed. Adjust row height as follows: 17.25 (23 pixels).

2. Place the columns used to compute the amount of change and percent of change to the right of the existing table values.

3. Change the title of the table to 20-point Book Antiqua Bold. (If Book Antiqua is not available, substitute another appropriate font.) Merge and center the title of the table across the width of the table. Change the title font color to red. Change the fill color to sky blue or light blue if these colors are available.

4. Revise the font and fill colors for the table, keeping the fill color for the column headings slightly darker than the color for the values in the table. Experiment until the best color combination is found.

5. Place the clip art image between the heading and the first line of the table. Format the clip art so that it appears aligned with the right side of the table. Resize the image as needed so that it is an appropriate size relative to the table.

6. Delete the rows containing the introductory text.

7. Format numbers so that commas are aligned. Right-align numeric entries in the table, but center-align column titles.

8. The text indicating the source of the table notation should be in boldface italics. Place a double line on the bottom border of the cells immediately above the source notation.

9. Add our company name at the bottom of the workbook, but hide the row so that it will not be visible to the viewer.

10. After the table is saved as a Web page, use the browser to open the file and view how the table will appear on the site.

11. Save the file in both workbook and Web page formats.

12. Surf the Internet to locate a site that can be used as a hyperlink. A suggested layout is shown at right. The graphic and hyperlink notation should be placed in a table. For the border setting, select None, so that borders do not display around the image.

Click to access additional career information.

• • • Job Planning Form • • •

Client: _____ Project: _____ Job: _____

1. What deliverables does the client expect for this job? (Examples include letter, printed report, slide presentation, database file, template, spreadsheet.)

2. Which additional resources, if any, do you need in finding information to complete the job? (Examples include Internet searches and documents on disk.)

3. What software do you need to complete this job?

4. What special software formatting features does the job call for?

STUDENT LOG

Name: _____ Date/Time Completed: _____

Document File Name(s): _____

Comments:

Client: ___State Community College Association___ Project: ___p2j1___

Job #1

Files Needed
sappaper.doc

Elsie Dickerson has been selected to make a presentation at the Global Information and Management Conference in Hawaii. She has developed a paper relating to SAP implementation that will be published in the conference proceedings, and she wants Ronald Powell to prepare it in final form. Along with her paper, Elsie gave Ronald the conference submission guidelines she had received. She asked that he carefully adhere to the guidelines and provide her with a printed copy of the revised paper. The guidelines and paper follow.

Client: **State Community College Association**   Project: **p2j1**

The paper should be prepared using Microsoft Word
GUIDELINES FOR AUTHORS

PAPER SIZE

The length of the paper is limited to four pages including the abstract, figures, tables, and references. This is a strict limit—no exceptions. Include a word count at the end of the paper.

PAPER FORMAT

Page Setup

Use 8.5" x 11" paper size. The margins should be 1" all around (top, bottom, left, right). Use a single column (do NOT use two columns). Pages should be numbered at the upper-right corner margin. The following notation should be placed in a footer and centered horizontally at the bottom of each page: **Hawaii GIMC.**

Font Face/Size

Select the Times New Roman font face. Set the font size to 10 pts.

Title

The title of the paper should be centered, bold, and in all CAPs.

Author Information

Provide author information immediately after the title. Use commas to separate the following information: name, affiliation, e-mail, and phone number. Information for each author is limited to one line.

Abstract

Include an abstract at the beginning of the paper; limit it to 150 words or less.

Paragraphs

Paragraphs should be fully justified (both left and right) and single-spaced throughout the paper. Allow one blank line after each paragraph. DO NOT indent the first line of paragraphs.

Headings

Allow one blank line after the first- and second-level headings. First-level headings should be centered, bold, and in all CAPs. Second-level headings should be centered, bold, and in title case (only the first character of the word is capitalized). Third-level headings should be left-aligned, bold, italicized, and in title case.

Figures and Tables

Keep figures and tables in close proximity to where they are mentioned in the body of the paper.

References

References should be shown as endnotes. Attempt to minimize the number of references. If necessary, invite readers to contact the author(s) for a complete list of references.

Client: **State Community College Association**   Project: **p2j1**

SAP Implementation Design

Elsie Dickerson
Director of Operations
State Community College Association
10047 Bennington Avenue
Kansas City, MO 64125

Abstract

SAP implementation affects most, if not all, of the company's business processes. Implementation models that worked well in the past may not be successful in today's client-centered environment. The integrative nature of SAP impacts the entire organization—all the way from the production process to the office of the top executive. A model for implementation must involve all of the stakeholders in the organization with a strong foundation required for successful implementation throughout the organization. This research includes a study of the methods, factors, and procedures that a multinational organization utilized while implementing SAP as its enterprise software program.

SAP: Enterprise Software Program

SAP (Systems, Applications, and Products in Data Processing) is an enterprise software program that requires integration of business processes. SAP was founded in 1972 in Waldorf, Germany, with a goal of becoming a global leader for providing client/server business applications. More than 8,000 companies in over 50 countries have chosen SAP client/server applications as their enterprise software provider.

The overall scope of SAP that was utilized by International Paper is shown below. Each of the modules can be implemented individually, which provides the enterprise with options that best suit its goals, objectives, timeline, and personnel.

Client: _____State Community College Association_____ Project: _____p2j1_____

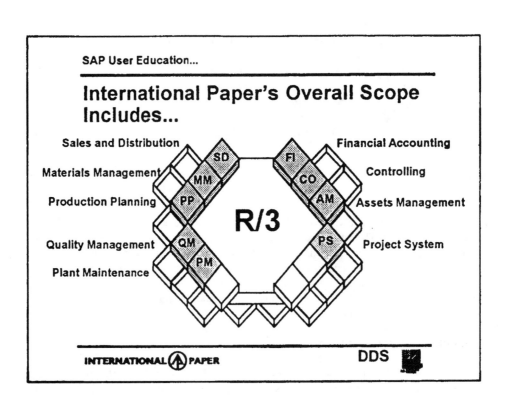

Pilot Implementation

The first stage in the model included a pilot implementation into one of the business units, Kraft Retail, which was owned by the corporation. Kraft was in a position in which it could not afford to implement SAP without corporate financial support. This provided a win-win situation: Kraft was getting a financial resource that it could not otherwise have afforded, and International Paper was provided with a vehicle for piloting the SAP program on a test basis, requiring a lower commitment of resources before implementation in other business units.

SAP systems that were implemented at Kraft during the pilot stage are shown below.

Kraft Packaging SAP Implementation Scope

• Sales and Distribution	• Financial Accounting
• Materials Management	• Controlling
• Production Planning	• Assets Management
• Project System	

Client: **State Community College Association** Project: **p2j1**

Kraft provided many hours to the project as the corporate pilot installation. International Paper provided financial investment and time commitment by the Information Technology group. Kraft got its information system and International Paper got the financial interface that it needed along with critical experience in SAP implementation.

Module Implementation

Financial modules provided the easiest implementation process. Reviews and analysis from the Information Technology group provided information that could be used to provide a critical capability for implementing SAP into the financial modules and into the next implementation modules—manufacturing and logistics.

Much of the information that was learned during the implementation of one module appeared to be applicable toward implementing other modules. This allowed for less reliance on outside consultants, which substantially reduced the cost of implementation.

Assessment and Planning

A review of the technology infrastructure that supports business units is a key ingredient to successful evaluation of an enterprise software program. This process helps to ensure that technicians and procedures are available to ensure that all hardware, software, and network components are properly evaluated, designed, and implemented.

SAP was chosen as the enterprise software program for several reasons. The primary reason was that the software fit with the redesigned best practices financial processes of the organization. The software was configurable to meet the company's vision. Also, the program received high scores when compared with competitive products relative to the following areas:

- Enterprise vs. division
- Fully integrated vs. interfaced
- Process vs. functional modularity
- Better support for supply chain
- Better integration of business processes
- Better access to information

Business Design and Prototype

The blueprint of the SAP project at International Paper incorporated many techniques, procedures, and resources into the project design. However, SAP's architectural features and the need to integrate the software into the structural design were critical considerations. This methodology was enhanced to support implementation of the R/3 version of SAP, which is the

Client: _State Community College Association_ Project: _p2j1_

client/server version. Prototyping and piloting can confirm how R/3 will best be implemented into the business and technology environment. The SAP Reference Model shown below provided documentation and a reference model to show prototyping, implementation procedures, and case studies.

Events, chains, activities, and work process can be optimized and compared to the reference model while using workflow tools. Early prototyping, using the configuration management tools from the workflow environment and the workflow editor, can be used with the reference model. SAP is the first software vendor to publish the structure of its software in modules that can be used by the user. Key business

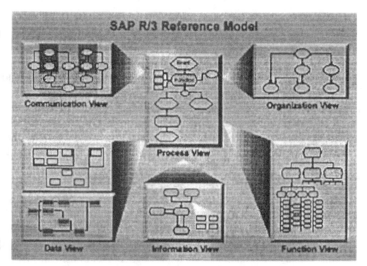

elements in the model are shown as business objects. R/3 has 160 business objects and 800 business processes. These objects—purchase orders or sales orders, for example—have their internal data models that provide a picture of what a model object (such as a customer order) should look like in R/3. With the connection of events and tasks, even very complex business processes can be clearly modeled and analyzed. Structure of the object in the Data Dictionary is also provided.

Testing and Training

Testing and training are key ingredients in the implementation model. The quality of education as well as the perception of end users toward the program can dramatically influence acceptance of new paradigms associated with program implementation.

Change Management

An important component of the implementation model was to anticipate, evaluate, and manage relevant cultural and organizational adjustments during all phases of system implementation. Re-engineering of business processes was required as decisions were being made about appropriate settings. Continuous organizational change must be viewed as a normal process for the organization.

Client: **State Community College Association**　　Project: **p2j1**

SAP is an integrated product that is being used throughout the organization. Therefore, each department must have knowledge about operations in other departments. End users do have to be experts, but they must know how their activities interact with the activities of other departments.

A key ingredient of change management is the ability to accommodate continuous change. IT models are in a state of constant change and require new configurations on a regular basis to respond to factors such as company growth, changing market conditions, customer demands, pressures from the competition, and technological innovations.

A change management team was an integral part of the implementation model. This team was responsible for assisting business units with building the infrastructure required to support the implementation model. The role of the change management team in the implementation model is shown below.

Change Management Team's Role
• Knowledge Transfer
• User Education
• User Communication
• Training Administration
• Infrastructure for Ongoing Support

Teamwork is important for successful implementation of the model. As part of the change management strategy, each location, organization, or department will have a local SAP change management team that will have a site leader, a technical expert, a security administrator, and technical support personnel to provide network support that ensures local user ownership at every level.

The SAP home page provides additional information about SAP products and services. For additional information, the home page can be located at the following URL site address: http://www.sap.com.

Citations Used in the Study

Helmer, Olaf, "SAP Cases and Examples," *Journal of Technology*, 12:45, May–June, 2002.

Collaso, Soniko, "SAP Model Design and Implementation," *Journal of Electronics*, 22:21–23, June 23, 2001.

Mistry, Sauren, "SAP Prototyping Design," *Journal of Technology and Management*, 14:32–35, July 14, 1999.

• • • Job Planning Form • • •

Client: _____ Project:_____ Job: _____

1. What deliverables does the client expect for this job? (Examples include letter, printed report, slide presentation, database file, template, spreadsheet.)

2. Which additional resources, if any, do you need in finding information to complete the job? (Examples include Internet searches and documents on disk.)

3. What software do you need to complete this job?

4. What special software formatting features does the job call for?

STUDENT LOG

Name: _____ Date/Time Completed: _____

Document File Name(s): _____

Comments:

Business Technology Consultants
Project and Job Information

Client: _____State Community College Association_____ Project: _____p3j1_____

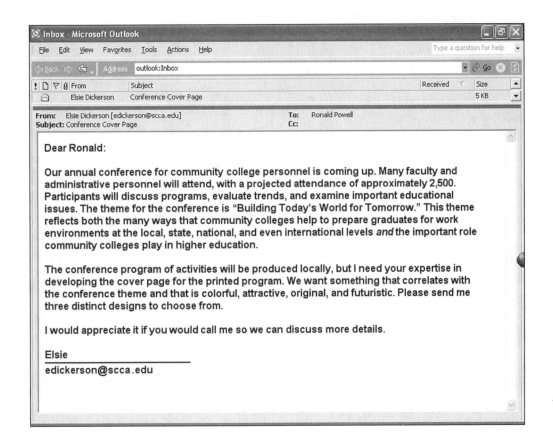

Job #1

Files Needed
None

Shortly after Ronald Powell received Elsie Dickerson's e-mail, he called her to discuss the cover to be developed. The program will be printed on 8.5" by 11" paper in a landscape orientation. Ronald has the option of using clip art or creating original artwork for the cover. Elsie recommended that he look on the Web to locate other conference program designs as examples. The name of the conference is 23rd Annual SCCA Conference. The location is the Downtown Inn, Seattle, Washington. The conference dates should be included on the cover; the meeting will be held on the last Friday, Saturday, and Sunday of the month that falls three months from the end of the present month.

3 diff coverpage

· · · Job Planning Form · · ·

Client: _____ Project:_____ Job: _____

1. What deliverables does the client expect for this job? (Examples include letter, printed report, slide presentation, database file, template, spreadsheet.)

2. Which additional resources, if any, do you need in finding information to complete the job? (Examples include Internet searches and documents on disk.)

3. What software do you need to complete this job?

4. What special software formatting features does the job call for?

STUDENT LOG

Name: _____ Date/Time Completed: _____

Document File Name(s): _____

Comments:

Client: State Community College Association   Project: p4j1

Job #1

NOTES

Files Needed
survey.doc

Recently BTC conducted a survey for SCCA to determine the reasons employers choose community colleges for workforce educational training. Results from the survey's 7,200 participants are now compiled. Elsie Dickerson needs this information presented in a short report with a table and bar chart that she can distribute at next week's Chamber of Commerce meeting. Elsie wants Ronald Powell to compose a one- or two-paragraph narrative to introduce and describe the primary results from the survey. She wants the narrative to be included in a Word document along with a reformatted two-column table created from a file she provided to Ronald. The table should include the following properties: table centered, grid borders, a light turquoise fill for shading, and a red font for characters. Tabs can be used as column separators, columns should be formatted to an appropriate width, and the title of the table should be centered. The bar chart should be embedded in the document. For the bar chart, Elsie wants the x-axis scale to show reasons and the y-axis scale to show percentages.

The table she provided is shown below. The numbers show how many participants chose each reason (participants were permitted to choose more than one).

**Reasons Employers Choose Community Colleges
For Workforce Education Training***

Cost Effectiveness	4,896
Customized Training Programs	3,816
Convenient Location	3,056
Quality of Instruction	2,740
Past Satisfaction with Results	2,024
Referred by Other Businesses	576
Other Reasons	360

*Source: Survey

Job Planning Form

Client: _____ Project: _____ Job: _____

1. What deliverables does the client expect for this job? (Examples include letter, printed report, slide presentation, database file, template, spreadsheet.)

2. Which additional resources, if any, do you need in finding information to complete the job? (Examples include Internet searches and documents on disk.)

3. What software do you need to complete this job?

4. What special software formatting features does the job call for?

STUDENT LOG

Name: _____ Date/Time Completed: _____

Document File Name(s): _____

Comments:

Client: **State Community College Association**   Project: **p5j1**

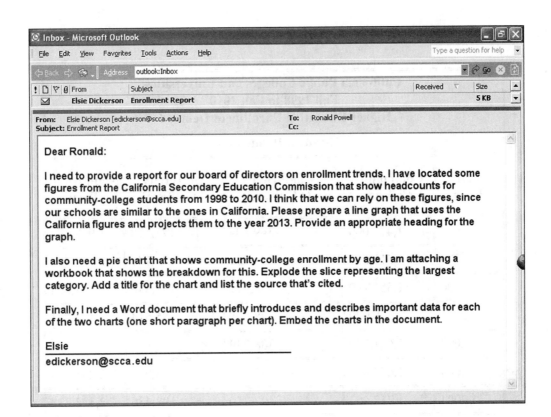

Job #1

Files Needed
student.doc
enrollment.xls

To provide the data BTC will need for the line graph, Elsie Dickerson later sent two files that will be needed to prepare the pie chart: one containing the California table so that data from the first two columns can be copied to a workbook, and another containing an Excel workbook. On the phone, she asked that each slice of the pie display in a different color. She also wants a pointer included in the chart that will connect the name of the category to the appropriate slice of the pie. (This eliminates any need for a legend.) The chart titles call for an attractive font and a shadow. Preceding each chart should be a sentence that introduces it plus another sentence that points out the most important characteristic it depicts. The table and additional data are presented on the following pages.

Client:_____State Community College Association_____ Project: _____p5j1_____

California Public Colleges and Universities Fall 1998 to Fall 2010 Higher Education Enrollment Demand Student Headcount				
Fall Term	Community Colleges	California State University	University of California	California Total
1998	1,475,000	349,804	173,570	1,998,374
1999	1,512,567	359,401	177,741	2,049,709
2000	1,551,199	368,919	181,546	2,101,664
2001	1,590,929	378,298	185,514	2,154,741
2002	1,631,790	388,039	189,692	2,209,521
2003	1,673,819	397,773	193,971	2,265,563
2004	1,717,052	407,750	198,436	2,323,238
2005	1,761,525	418,018	203,085	2,382,628
2006	1,807,279	429,568	207,980	2,444,827
2007	1,854,353	441,403	213,065	2,508,821
2008	1,902,789	453,388	218,395	2,574,572
2009	1,952,629	466,433	223,952	2,643,014
2010	2,003,918	479,485	229,724	2,713,127
Percent Change	35.86%	37.07%	32.35%	35.77%
Additional Students	528,918	129,681	56,154	714,753

Client: State Community College Association   Project: p5j1

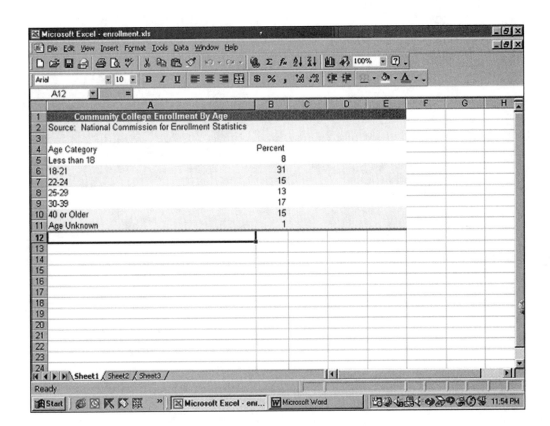

Job Planning Form

Client: _____ Project:_____ Job: _____

1. What deliverables does the client expect for this job? (Examples include letter, printed report, slide presentation, database file, template, spreadsheet.)

2. Which additional resources, if any, do you need in finding information to complete the job? (Examples include Internet searches and documents on disk.)

3. What software do you need to complete this job?

4. What special software formatting features does the job call for?

STUDENT LOG

Name: _____ Date/Time Completed: _____

Document File Name(s): _____

Comments:

Client: _____State Community College Association_____ Project: _____p6j1_____

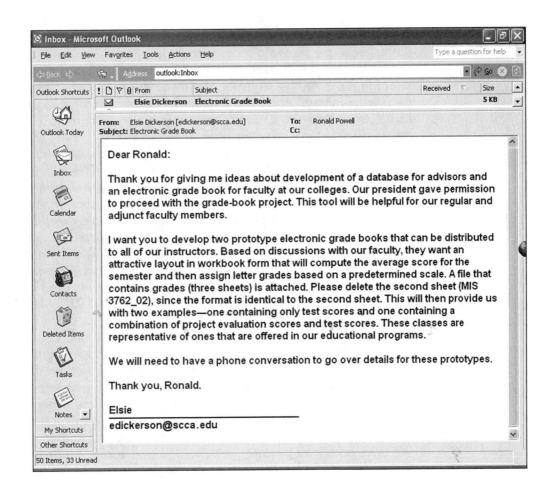

Client: ____State Community College Association____   Project: ____p6j1____

Job #1

Files Needed
grades.xls

Based on Elsie Dickerson's e-mail and accompanying file (the worksheets are shown on the next page), Ronald Powell understands that BTC needs to provide a formula to compute the average score for the semester and then assign a grade based on a table lookup procedure. Students in the first sample class complete six projects (P1 to P6) with a possibility of earning 100 points. The students complete three periodic tests (T1 to T3) with a possibility of earning 250 points. Students complete a final exam (T4) with a possibility of earning 100 points. The students complete an integrated project (Proj) with a possibility of earning 100 points. Missing project scores are awarded a score of zero.

In the follow-up phone conversation, Elsie told Ronald to assign the following weights while computing the course averages for the Multimedia Applications class: projects, 20 percent; periodic tests, 30 percent; final exam, 25 percent; and integrated project, 25 percent. She wants the lookup table that is used for assigning the final grade to be set up as follows: A, 91 to 100 percent; B, 81 to 90 percent; C, 71 to 80 percent; D, 61 to 70 percent; and F, 60 percent or below. Columns will need to be added to display the course average computation and final grade determination. She also wants to see the table lookup data that is used to assign the final grades.

BTC's research department provided sample data to permit a testing of the analysis used to determine the course average and final grade. Sample data indicates that Sandra Anderson will have an 81.52 percent class average and earn a grade of B in the MIS 3762_01 course. This can be used to test the formula and table lookup function for the Multimedia Applications course.

Similar analysis will be needed for the Microsoft® Office Applications course. Elsie indicated that the following weights should be used to compute the course average. Students completed three periodic tests (T1 to T3) with a possibility of 250 points. Students could earn 100 points on the project (P) and 100 points on the final exam (F). The following weights should be used: periodic tests, 35 percent; project, 40 percent; and final exam, 25 percent. This course will use the same scale that was used in the previous lookup table for assigning grades. Columns will need to be added to display the course average and grade for each student. If computations from the research department are correct, Fred Barczak will have an 82.97 course average and earn a grade of B in the course.

Client: State Community College Association Project: p6j1

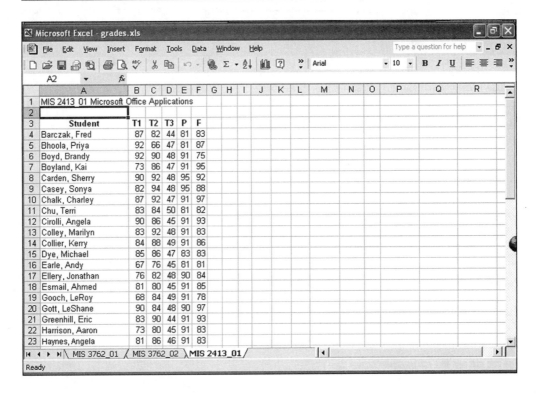

Client: _____State Community College Association_____ Project: _____p6j2_____

Job #2

Files Needed
None

Elsie requested that the minimum score, maximum score, and average score for each column be computed and placed at the bottom of the sheet for the Microsoft Office Applications course. She also requested that a column be added to the same sheet denoting that the student passed if the course average is 71 or higher and failed if the overall average is 70 or less. She indicated that a grade of C or higher is required in order to pass courses that are required in the major.

Completion of the following forms will be helpful while planning for this project. They will also provide documentation that will be useful for Elsie.

Business Technology Consultants
Project and Job Information

Client: State Community College Association   Project: p6j2

Multimedia Applications Formulas

Course average:	
Grade determination:	

Microsoft Office Application Formulas

Course average:	
Grade determination:	
Minimum score:	
Maximum score:	
Average score:	

Table Lookup Entry Scale

Location (Cell Address) of Table Lookup Values

Multimedia Applications:	
Microsoft Office Applications:	

Function Formula to Determine Course Failures

Microsoft Office Applications:	

• • • Job Planning Form • • •

Client: _____ Project: _____ Job: _____

1. What deliverables does the client expect for this job? (Examples include letter, printed report, slide presentation, database file, template, spreadsheet.)

2. Which additional resources, if any, do you need in finding information to complete the job? (Examples include Internet searches and documents on disk.)

3. What software do you need to complete this job?

4. What special software formatting features does the job call for?

STUDENT LOG

Name: _____ Date/Time Completed: _____

Document File Name(s): _____

Comments:

Client: **State Community College Association**   Project: **p6j3**

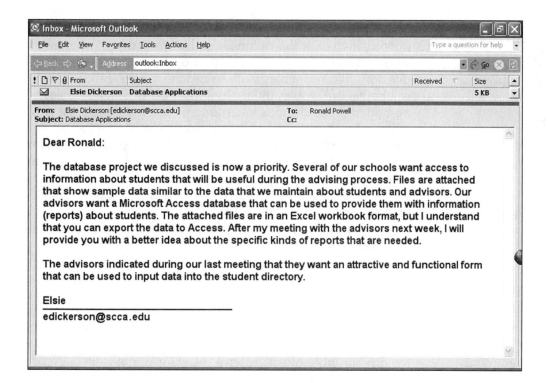

Client: **State Community College Association**　　Project: **p6j3**

Job #3

Files Needed
students.xls
advisors.xls

Elsie Dickerson and Ronald Powell discussed the project by phone. She wants the database to be created with a name that will be easily associated with the project, and suggested this: directory. The two tables that she attached to her e-mail message will be the only tables in the database, but additional tables can be added if she decides to expand the project. Since the two tables have a common field, data from them can be joined. After importing each of the two tables to the Access database, remove from each table any excess columns or rows that were created as a result of importing the workbook file.

Creation of the database can be initiated immediately. Elsie wants to enforce the following business rules:

1. Each student must have an advisor.
2. Each student has only one advisor.
3. Some advisors do not have to advise students.
4. Each advisor can be assigned to advise more than one student.

She indicated that a diagram is needed to illustrate the relationship between students and advisors established by these rules. It should include a rectangle for each of the two tables—the advisor table directly above the student table—in a Word or Publisher format. A single-point line should connect the two tables with the arrow pointing to the student table. Elsie requested a fill for the rectangle box. Place the actual name of each table (text box) inside the appropriate rectangle with a lighter color fill than was used for the rectangle. She suggested dark and light turquoise, but left the choice of color up to BTC as long as the fill for the rectangle includes a darker shade than the fill for the text box. A sample of what she wants is shown below. Include the following heading above the diagram in a 14-point font: Entity-Relational Diagram.

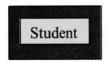

Business Technology Consultants
Project and Job Information

Client: State Community College Association   Project: p6j3

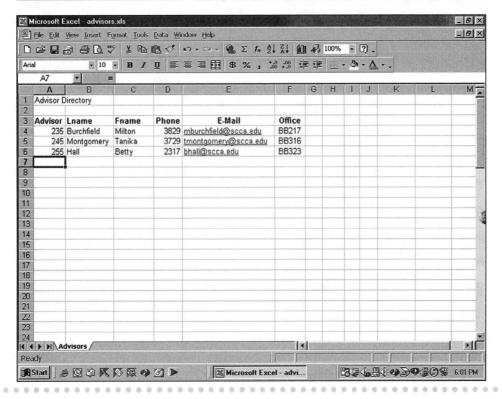

Client: **State Community College Association**   Project: **p6j4**

Job #4

Files Needed
None

Elsie called to provide a listing of the types of reports that are needed by the advisors. She requested printed sample reports for each query so that the advisors can see how these will appear in report format. Unless otherwise indicated, student names should appear in ascending order by last name and first name. Elsie's list, along with a form for preplanning the queries, follows. The grade point average will be a derived field with the formula included on the query form as needed.

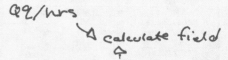

Notes on Report Types for SCCA Advisors

1. A listing of student ID, name, major, hours, quality points, grade point average, phone extension, e-mail address, advisor number, and advisor name.

2. A listing of all information in the student table for each student who is advised by Milton Burchfield.

3. A listing of the student ID, name, major, and grade point average for each student who has a grade point average that is equal to or greater than 3.5.

4. A listing of the student ID and name for all MIS majors.

5. A listing of the student ID and name for all MIS majors who have a grade point average that is equal to or greater than 3.5.

6. A listing of the student ID and name for all MIS or ACCT majors who have a grade point average that is equal to or greater than 3.0.

7. The name, phone number, e-mail address, and office number for the person who advises Ronnie Elliott.

8. A listing of each advisor's number and name along with the total number of persons who are advised by each advisor.

9. A listing of student ID, name, phone number, and advisor name for each student who has a grade point average that is below 2.0.

10. A listing of student ID and name for each student who is majoring in MIS and has completed 30 or more hours.

Client: _____State Community College Association_____ Project: _____p6j4_____

Query No.	Criteria Entered
1	
2	
3	
4	
5	
6	
7	
8	
9	
10	

Job Planning Form

Client: _____ Project:_____ Job: _____

1. What deliverables does the client expect for this job? (Examples include letter, printed report, slide presentation, database file, template, spreadsheet.)

2. Which additional resources, if any, do you need in finding information to complete the job? (Examples include Internet searches and documents on disk.)

3. What software do you need to complete this job?

4. What special software formatting features does the job call for?

STUDENT LOG

Name: _____ Date/Time Completed: _____

Document File Name(s): _____

Comments:

Client: _____State Community College Association_____ Project: _____p7j1_____

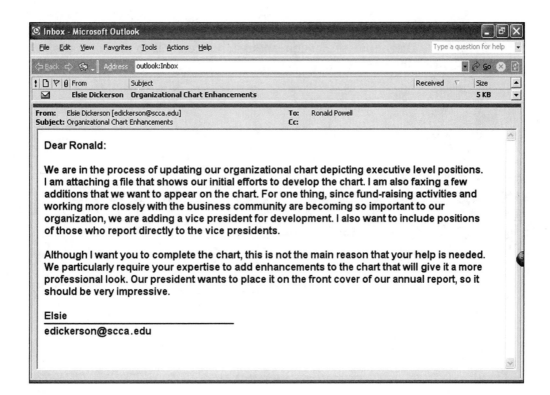

Client: _____State Community College Association_____ Project: _____p7j1_____

Job #1

Files Needed
org_chart.ppt

Below is the chart Elsie sent. Ronald's notes regarding their telephone discussion about enhancements to the chart are on the next page.

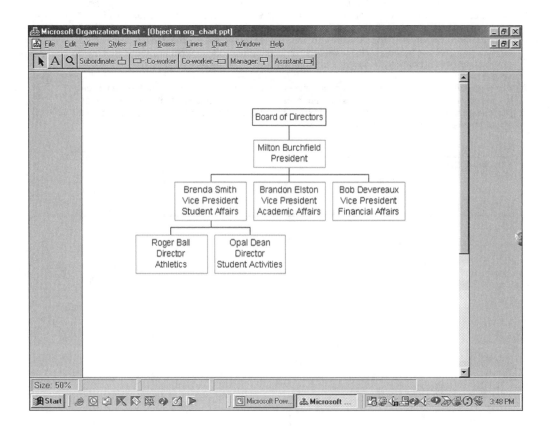

Client: __State Community College Association__ Project: ___p7j1___

Enhancements per phone conversation with Elsie Dickerson

1. Use customized WordArt to improve the appearance of the title, State Community College Association.

2. The adopted colors of the organization are blue and gray, so Elsie wants to incorporate these colors into the design scheme. She liked the idea of each box having a light gray background with the text in a boldface blue font.

3. The border around each box should also be blue.

4. Many of the association's brochures use turquoise as part of the color scheme, so Elsie prefers light turquoise for the chart background.

5. She suggested placing a shadow on the border for each box to create a more professional presentation.

Client: **State Community College Association**   Project: **p7j1**

Job #1
**(continued)
Files Needed**
org_chart.ppt

Elsie sent the following fax to suggest a revised structure that includes the additional positions. The vice president for development will be on the same level as the other vice presidents. Each of the three deans will report to Brandon Elston. The director of accounting will report to Bob Devereaux. The directors of outreach and fundraising will report to Dana Margola.

Fax to: *Ronald Powell*
Fax from: *Elsie Dickerson*
Subject: *Organizational Chart Additions*

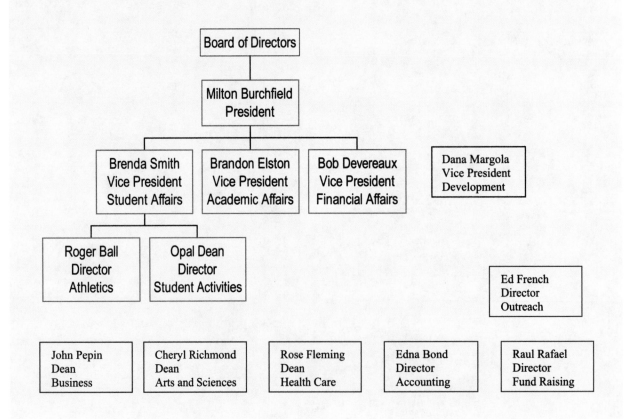

Business
Technology
Consultants

• • • Job Planning Form • • •

Client: _____ Project:_____ Job: _____

1. What deliverables does the client expect for this job? (Examples include letter, printed report, slide presentation, database file, template, spreadsheet.)

2. Which additional resources, if any, do you need in finding information to complete the job? (Examples include Internet searches and documents on disk.)

3. What software do you need to complete this job?

4. What special software formatting features does the job call for?

STUDENT LOG

Name: _____ Date/Time Completed: _____

Document File Name(s): _____

Comments:

Client:_____State Community College Association_____ Project: _____p8j1_____

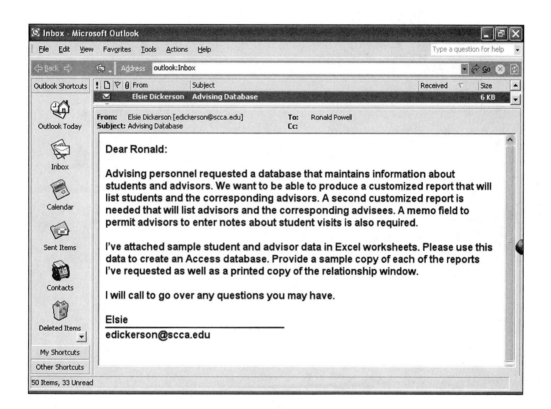

Job #1

Files Needed
students.xls
advisors.xls

When Elsie Dickerson called Ronald Powell to discuss the job, she told him that an advisor can advise many students, but each student has only one advisor. It will be necessary to add a field to establish this relationship. Elsie also mentioned that referential integrity should be established to ensure that each advisor number entered in the student table represents a valid advisor number in the advisor table. The sample data are shown on the next page.

Note: The database used for Project 6, Job 3, if completed and saved on disk, can be used for completing the activities Elsie has requested for this job. Otherwise, the Excel files listed above (and used in Project 6, Job 3) can be imported to develop the Access database.

Business Technology Consultants
Project and Job Information

Client: _____State Community College Association_____ Project: _____p8j1_____

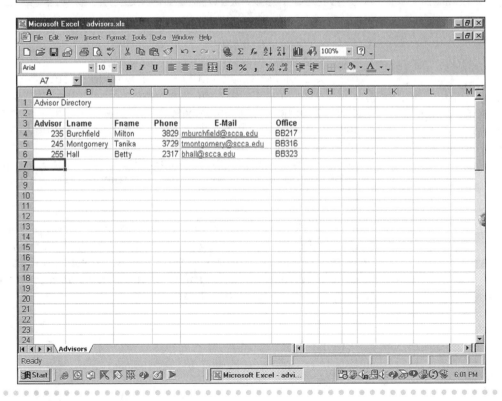

Job Planning Form

Client: _____ Project: _____ Job: _____

1. What deliverables does the client expect for this job? (Examples include letter, printed report, slide presentation, database file, template, spreadsheet.)

2. Which additional resources, if any, do you need in finding information to complete the job? (Examples include Internet searches and documents on disk.)

3. What software do you need to complete this job?

4. What special software formatting features does the job call for?

STUDENT LOG

Name: _____ Date/Time Completed: _____

Document File Name(s): _____

Comments:

CLIENT 4 Runyan Management Services
Projects Overview

Runyan Management Services (RMS) is a privately held company that leases and manages office buildings in seven states with the home office located in Boston, Massachusetts. Bobby Runyan, President and Chief Operating Officer, started the company in 1963 in Memphis, Tennessee. The firm uses cutting-edge technology and best practice processes to meet changing customer needs and to fulfill or exceed industry standards. Along with its integrated approach to the management of real estate properties in the commercial market, RMS provides a full range of leasing services to property owners.

This clear focus has permitted the company to maintain a leading role in the industry.

The corporate strategy is to combine commitment and service with professionalism to deliver services to customers on time, every time—an approach that has permitted the company to become one of the top property management providers in the commercial real estate market. The RMS goal is to deliver superior services in an efficient manner and with greater economies of scale to customers. Offering better opportunities to its employees helps the firm recruit and retain the best sales and marketing professionals in the business.

Services Requested

RMS maintains a close relationship with Business Technology Consultants (BTC). Business documents used by the company must be properly designed to be both functional and attractive in order to meet the needs of clients and real estate professionals. The company depends on BTC to use its extensive graphic arts department to design document layouts and develop forms that help to maintain its stellar image. Ketaki Cheema, director of development and finance, has responsibility for coordinating activities with Ronald Powell, who is the contact person at BTC. At present, Ronald is consulting on eight projects:

- **Project 1** (three jobs) involves creating, formatting, and testing three different Excel forms: an expense report, a form for recording lease commissions, and a lease availability report.

- **Project 2** (two jobs) calls for creating a vehicle for entering variables into a mail-merge lease agreement along with a Web-based schedule of payments on leases.

- **Project 3** (one job) requires the development of a chart template showing transaction timelines so potential customers can see what to expect if they contract with RMS to manage a new office facility.

- **Project 4** (one job), a statistical report about the office-building market in one RMS business region, calls for creating Excel charts, incorporating them into a written report, and formatting the report.

- **Project 5** (two jobs) requires creating two colorful, illustrated advertising flyers, one for sales properties and one for rental properties.

- **Project 6** (one job) is a detailed revision of a PowerPoint slide presentation that includes charts and a multimedia movie slide.

- **Project 7** (one job) involves work on another, more detailed PowerPoint slide show and conversion from slides to a Word document that RMS will present to an important client.

- **Project 8** (one job) calls for adjusting properties in an Excel workbook of property listings, using the data to prepare a customized form and report, and exporting the files into an Access database.

Client: _____ Runyan Management Services _____ Project: _____ p1j1 _____

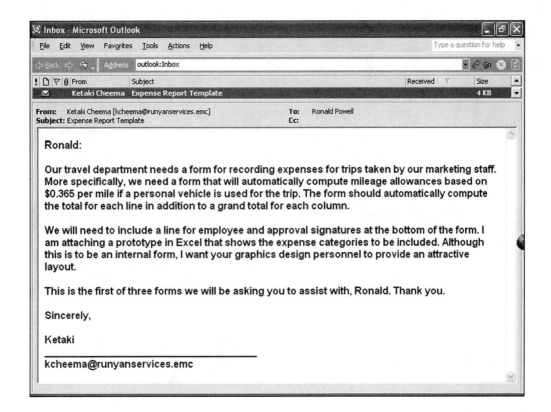

Client: _____Runyan Management Services_____ Project: _____p1j1_____

Job #1

Files Needed
expense.xls

The form Ketaki Cheema provided is shown below. When she and Ronald Powell spoke on the phone, she explained that she wants to receive a file on disk and a printed copy for both the template and a version of the template with sample data entered to test the process. Tony Burdette, BTC's graphic arts design specialist, reviewed the expense report project and made several recommendations for the form, which are listed on the next page.

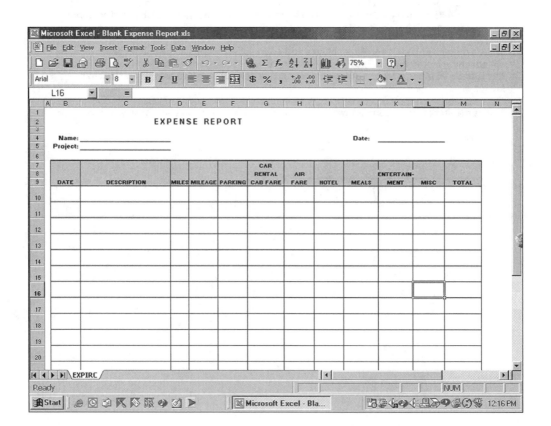

Client: **Runyan Management Services**   Project: **p1j1**

Specifications/recommendations assume that cell addresses are the same as in the sample.

1. Adjust heights for rows 1 through 9 to an appropriate measure—something near 12.75 (17 pixels). Remove inside borders for the range of cells on rows 7 to 9. Then add outside borders only for this range.

2. Adjust heights for rows 10 and below to an appropriate measure—something near 24.75 (33 pixels).

3. Add a function at the top of the form so that the date will automatically be entered when the form is accessed.

4. Add an appropriate fill and font color for the column headings, rows 7 through 9.

5. Adjust column widths as appropriate for the types of data that will be entered.

6. Add a formula to compute the mileage amount in column E, based on the number of miles times the mileage rate. For the purpose of this template, assume $0.365 as the mileage rate. Add a formula to compute the horizontal total in column M. Add formulas for each appropriate column on the last row to compute a vertical total for the column. Add an appropriate label for the last row.

7. Place borders around all cells in the table as shown in the prototype layout.

8. A label and space for signatures can be placed below the last row of the table. Bottom borders can be placed in the cells above each signature label to provide lines for the signatures.

9. The signature labels should be similar to the design shown below.

_____   _____
            Employee Signature   *Approval Signature*

10. The finished worksheet will serve as an expense report template for Runyan Management Services.

Job Planning Form

Client: _____ Project:_____ Job: _____

1. What deliverables does the client expect for this job? (Examples include letter, printed report, slide presentation, database file, template, spreadsheet.)

2. Which additional resources, if any, do you need in finding information to complete the job? (Examples include Internet searches and documents on disk.)

3. What software do you need to complete this job?

4. What special software formatting features does the job call for?

STUDENT LOG

Name: _____ Date/Time Completed: _____

Document File Name(s): _____

Comments:

Business Technology Consultants
Project and Job Information

Client: _____Runyan Management Services_____ Project: _____p1j2_____

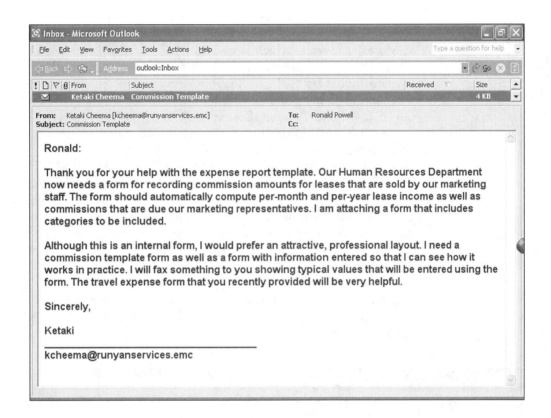

Client: **Runyan Management Services** Project: **p1j2**

Job #2

Files Needed
commission.xls

Ketaki Cheema faxed this additional information: The property is Majestic Towers, which is owned by JRT Enterprises, 1985 Shore Drive, St. Petersburg, FL 31706. Correspondence and invoice should be sent c/o Runyan Management Services to the attention of Jenny Bottoms. The tenant is Broadway Productions, 2416 Townsend Avenue, Boston, MA 02176. This is a new lease for 3,468 square feet for a term of 48 months. The lease will run from 12/1/2003 to 11/30/2007.

Per-square-foot charge will be as follows: year 1, $18.00; year 2, $18.25; year 3, $18.50; year 4, $18.75. Since some leases run for as long as ten years, the template should include space on the form and appropriate formulas to accommodate a lease of that length, even though test data covers only four years. For this prototype, Ketaki wants BTC to use a 4-percent commission rate.

Tony Burdette reviewed this project and made recommendations. Following are the commission form prototype, Tony's guidelines, and a form he provided for recording the formulas.

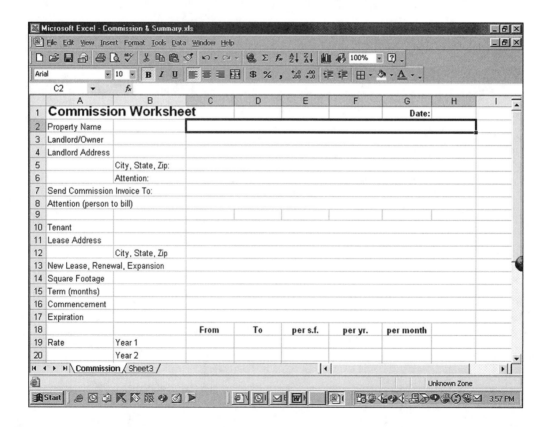

Client: _____ Runyan Management Services _____ Project: _____ p1j2 _____

Notes for RMS Commission Lease Form—T. Burdette

1. The title font should be in an appropriate color and in a larger font size. The current date should display automatically each time the worksheet is accessed. Cell borders should be removed from the area where the above items are located on the worksheet.

2. Vertical cell borders should be removed except as shown on the prototype. Both vertical and horizontal cell borders should be removed from the section that lists the years.

3. Appropriate fill and font colors should be used to highlight the area that separates property information from tenant information. This feature is illustrated in the prototype.

4. Appropriate fill and font colors should be used to highlight the entire row containing the total commission amount.

5. An enlarged, dark red border should be placed around the entire worksheet with the exception of the top row(s) containing the title and date.

6. Page Setup properties should be adjusted to accommodate the desired print scheme.

Formula Planning Form

Cell Address	Purpose	Formula
F19	Rental per Year	
G19	Rental per Month	
F29	Total Rental	
C31	Total Commission	

Job Planning Form

Client: _____ Project:_____ Job: _____

1. What deliverables does the client expect for this job? (Examples include letter, printed report, slide presentation, database file, template, spreadsheet.)

2. Which additional resources, if any, do you need in finding information to complete the job? (Examples include Internet searches and documents on disk.)

3. What software do you need to complete this job?

4. What special software formatting features does the job call for?

STUDENT LOG

Name: _____ Date/Time Completed: _____

Document File Name(s): _____

Comments:

Client: _____Runyan Management Services_____ Project: ____p1j3____

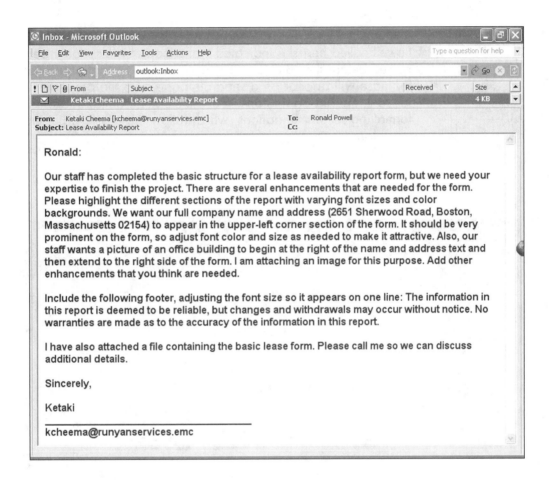

Client: Runyan Management Services   Project: p1j3

Job #3

Files Needed
lease.xls
office.gif

Below is the form Ketaki Cheema included. When Ronald Powell called her, she indicated that a page break should be placed before the "Buildings for Sale" section so that properties for lease will appear on a separate page from the properties for sale. Ronald again consulted with Tony Burdette regarding formatting recommendations, which follow the prototype of the lease form.

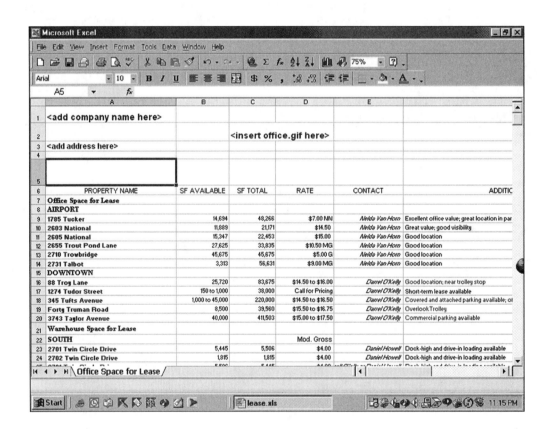

Client: _____ Runyan Management Services _____ Project: _____ p1j3 _____

Notes from Tony and Ronald's Conversation

1. Insert the name of the company in a text box near the upper-left side of the form. Use a boldface font for the name.

2. Insert the address of the company in a text box immediately below the name of the company. The address font should be smaller than the one for the company name.

3. White fill and blue font colors are recommended for both of the above text boxes.

4. The company name, address, and graphic image should be placed on the first five rows since the column headings begin on row 6. Row heights may need adjustments to make this possible.

5. Size adjustments should be made, as needed, to assure that all of the space above row 6 is utilized for the text boxes and graphic image. Horizontal space allocated for the text boxes should be one-third to one-fourth of the available space across the form.

6. All headings on the form should appear in the same font style—perhaps Futura Md BT if available—though size should vary according to importance of the heading. The font size used for property listings should be smaller than the one for headings.

7. Fill and font color selections should also vary according to the importance of the heading but should be used consistently throughout the form.

8. Use a text box to place the following text on top of the image that was inserted at the top of the form: Lease Bi-Monthly Availability Report. Font size and color for the text in the box should be appropriate to attract attention and still fit into the space.

9. Freeze the horizontal pane after row 6 so that the column headings will remain on the screen at all times.

10. Adjust the sheet header, if needed, so that the first six rows of the form will be printed on all pages.

11. Use a landscape page orientation, if needed, so that all columns can be printed on the same sheet.

12. Format the column headings to appear in italics and boldface.

13. The image Ketaki provided is stored in "gif" format and was sent with the basic lease form draft.

Business Technology Consultants

● ● ● **Job Planning Form** ● ● ●

Client: _____ Project: _____ Job: _____

1. What deliverables does the client expect for this job? (Examples include letter, printed report, slide presentation, database file, template, spreadsheet.)

2. Which additional resources, if any, do you need in finding information to complete the job? (Examples include Internet searches and documents on disk.)

3. What software do you need to complete this job?

4. What special software formatting features does the job call for?

STUDENT LOG

Name: _____ Date/Time Completed: _____

Document File Name(s): _____

Comments:

Client: _____Runyan Management Services_____ Project: _____p2j1_____

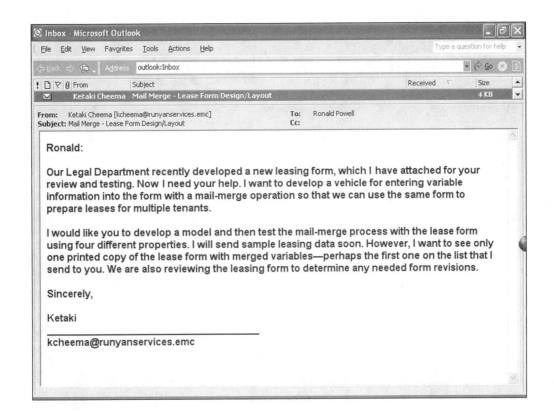

Job #1

NOTES

Files Needed
lease.doc
lease_variable.xls

While waiting for the sample data, Ronald Powell asked Tony Burdette to review the lease form. By the time Ketaki Cheema sent the sample test data, Tony had prepared an Excel list of lease variables for the workbook that will be used to merge data with the lease form. Column widths, formats, and so forth will need adjusting after data are entered in the workbook. The variables and sample data are on the following pages, followed by additional information from Ketaki along with the main lease agreement document.

Client: __Runyan Management Services__ Project: __p2j1__

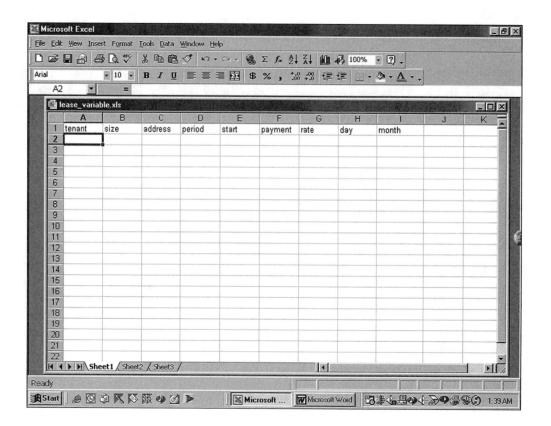

Business Technology Consultants
Project and Job Information

Client: Runyan Management Services   Project: p2j1

Sample Data from Ketaki

tenant: Massachusetts State Bank size: 8,933 address: 2506 Montrose Street period: 10 (ten) start: February 10, 200X payment: $17,980 rate: 6 (six) day: 12th month: January	tenant: B and H Enterprises size: 7,945 address: 4124 Hollywood Road period: 20 (twenty) start: June 1, 200X payment: $15,950 rate: 7 (seven) day: 1st month: May
tenant: Dover Construction Company size: 6,933 address: 3528 Jefferson Circle period: 20 (twenty) start: November 15, 200X payment: $16,980 rate: 6 (six) day: 10th month: October	tenant: Modern Electronic Design size: 8,423 address: 3214 Orchard Road period: 15 (fifteen) start: April 1, 200X payment: $19,420 rate: 5 (five) day: 3rd month: March

Client: _____ Runyan Management Services _____ Project: _____ p2j1 _____

Job #1

(continued)
Files Needed
lease.doc
lease_variable.xls

The lease form main document can be used for coding during the merge process. Merge variable locations are indicated on the form by comments that Tony placed inside caret brackets (< >) to coincide with the workbook merge variables.

Ketaki requested that two corrections be made to the main document: First, add the letter "s" to the end of the word "material" near the end of the second item. Second, add the following sentence to the end of the second item: Tenant shall have a right to cancel this lease upon the tenth (10th) anniversary of the lease term, so long as Tenant gives written notice at least six (6) months prior to the end of the requested lease termination date.

In addition, she requested that the Track Changes option be selected (without a password being added) so that she can verify that the changes were made to the form.

Client: _____ Runyan Management Services _____ Project: _____ p2j1 _____

LEASE AGREEMENT

THIS LEASE AGREEMENT (the "Lease") is made and entered into by and between RUNYAN MANAGEMENT SERVICES (the "Landlord") and **\<insert tenant here\>** (the "Tenant").

WITNESSETH:

1.   Leased Premises. Landlord hereby leases to Tenant, and Tenant hereby leases from Landlord approximately **\<insert size here\>** square feet of Rentable Area, as hereinafter defined, on portions of floor one (1) in **\<insert address here\>** (the "Building") located in Boston, Massachusetts. Tenant shall have the right to use the common areas of the Building and have all necessary rights of access to the Leased Premises.

2.   Term. The term ("Term") of this Lease shall be for a period of **\<insert period here\>** years and shall commence on the earlier of: (a) **\<insert start here\>** or (b) such other date as Tenant actually occupies the Leased Premises. Payments will be made in monthly installments payable in advance on or before the first day of each calendar month in the amount of **\<insert payment here\>**, which shall be increased by **\<insert rate here\>** percent each year during the term on the lease. In addition to the Base Rental, Tenant agrees to pay to Landlord all charges for any services, goods, or material furnished by Landlord at Tenant's request.

3.   Parking. Any parking permits for parking spaces shall be provided solely for the accommodation of Tenant for no additional costs throughout the term of the lease. Tenant (including Tenant's employees, agents, invitees, and visitors) will use the parking spaces solely for the purpose of parking passenger model cars, small vans, and small trucks, and will comply in all respects with any rules and regulations that may be promulgated by Landlord from time to time with respect to the parking areas.

4.   Use. The Leased Premises shall be used and occupied by Tenant solely for general office and retail purposes or any other use allowed under the current zoning regulations. Tenant will not bring any animals (except "Seeing Eye" dogs) or birds into the Building, and will not permit bicycles or other vehicles inside or on the sidewalks outside the Building except in areas designated from time to time by Landlord for such purposes. Canvassing, peddling, soliciting, and distributing handbills or any other written materials in the Building are prohibited, and each Tenant will cooperate to prevent the same. No cooking will be done or permitted by any Tenant on the Premises, except in areas of the Premises which are specially constructed for cooking and except that use by the Tenant of microwave ovens and Underwriters' Laboratory approved equipment for brewing coffee, tea, hot chocolate, and similar beverages will be permitted, provided that such use is in accordance with all applicable federal, state, and city laws, codes, ordinances, rules, and regulations.

Client:_____ Runyan Management Services _____ Project: _____ p2j1 _____

5.   Improvement of Leased Premises. The Leased Premises shall be prepared for the occupancy of Tenant in accordance with the provisions of the Work Letter Agreement between Landlord and Tenant.

6.   Acceptance of Leased Premises and Building by Tenant. The taking of possession of the Leased Premises by Tenant shall be conclusive evidence as against Tenant that it accepts the Leased Premises as suitable for the purpose for which same are leased.

(A) Landlord agrees to furnish for the occupied portion of the Leased Premises the following services: (i) air conditioning, both heating and cooling (as required by the seasons) from approximately 7:30 a.m. to 6:00 p.m. on Monday through Friday. Tenant shall have access to Tenant's space twenty-four (24) hours a day, seven (7) days a week.

(B) Landlord shall furnish sufficient power for lighting and for typewriters, calculating machines, personal computers, word processing machines, and other machines of similar low electrical consumption that are common in standard business offices, but not including electricity for computers and/or electronic data processing equipment and special lighting in excess of Building Standard.

7.   Maintenance and Repairs by Landlord. Subject to the provisions of this Lease, Landlord shall provide for the cleaning, painting, and maintenance of the public portions of the Property, including landscaping surrounding the Building in keeping with the usual standard for first-class office buildings located in the business district. Landlord will, at Tenant's written request, maintain any Leasehold Improvement that is Not Building Standard, such as hardwood floors, at Tenant's cost, plus an additional charge of fifteen percent (15%) of such cost to cover the overhead costs of Landlord's manager.

8.   Entry for Inspection and Repair. Landlord, its officers, agents, and representatives shall have the right, with prior notice to Tenant, to enter all parts of the Leased Premises (with the exception of designated security area) at all reasonable hours, and in the event of an emergency at any time.

9.   Repairs and Care of Property by Tenant. Tenant agrees at its own cost and expense to repair or replace any damage or injury done to the Building, or any part thereof, caused by Tenant, Tenant's agents, employees, or visitors.

10. Alterations, Additions, Improvements. Tenant shall not use or permit the Leased Premises to be used for any unlawful purpose. Tenant shall be entitled to make minor alterations such as placing items on the walls of the Leased Premises so long as once they are removed, Tenant repairs any damage caused thereby.

Client: _____ Runyan Management Services _____ Project: _____ p2j1 _____

11. Furniture, Fixtures, and Personal Property. Tenant may, at Tenant's sole cost and expense, remove its trade fixtures, office supplies, and movable office furniture and equipment not attached to the Building, provided: (a) such removal is made within ten (10) days after the termination of the Term of this Lease; and (b) Tenant is not in default of any obligation or covenant under this Lease at the time of such removal.

12. Taxes on Tenant's Property. Tenant shall be liable for all taxes levied or assessed against personal property, furniture, or fixtures placed by Tenant in the Leased Premises.

13. Insurance. Landlord shall, during the Term, obtain and keep in force: (i) comprehensive general liability insurance coverage in an amount not less than $2,000,000.00; and (ii) fire and extended coverage insurance in an amount not less than ninety percent (90%) of the full replacement cost of the Building (not including any Tenant's property or leasehold improvements paid for by Tenant).

14. Events of Default. The following events shall be deemed to be events of default by Tenant under this Lease: Tenant shall fail to comply with any term, provision, or covenant of this Lease (other than the payment of Rent) or of the Work Letter Agreement between Landlord and Tenant, and shall not cure such failure within thirty (30) days after written notice thereof to Tenant.

15. Attorneys' Fees. Upon any breach by either party of any of its obligations under this Lease, the other party, if not in breach, shall be entitled to recover all expenses including reasonable attorneys' fees incurred in connection with any breach.

16. Tenant's Right to Terminate Lease. Tenant currently holds a first mortgage loan (the "Mortgage") on the Property. Landlord agrees that Landlord will not replace the Mortgage with mortgage financing obtained from another bank or institutional lender during the Term of this Lease unless at the scheduled maturity of the Mortgage or any extension or refinancing of the Mortgage.

IN WITNESS WHEREOF, Landlord and Tenant, acting herein by duly authorized individuals, have caused this Lease to be executed as of the **\<insert day here\>** day of **\<insert month here\>**, 200X.

TENANT: LANDLORD:
\<insert tenant here\> RUNYAN MANAGEMENT SERVICES

Client: _____ Runyan Management Services _____ Project: _____ p2j1 _____

By: _____   By: _____

Title: _____   Title: _____

<Insert an automatic (forced) page break here>

WORK LETTER AGREEMENT

_____, 200X

_____
_____
_____
_____

    Re: Lease of **<insert size here>** square feet of Rentable Area located at **<insert address here>**, Boston, Massachusetts.

Dear Lessee:

    <insert tenant here> (hereinafter collectively referred to as "Tenant") and RUNYAN MANAGEMENT SERVICES (hereinafter referred to as "Landlord") are executing, simultaneously with this Work Letter Agreement (herein so called), a written lease covering the space referred to above (hereinafter called the "Leased Premises").

    1.   <u>Space Planning.</u>

    1.01.   Landlord's designated space planner, at no cost to Tenant, will prepare a space plan for the Leased Premises showing the location of all Building Standard partitions and doors.

    1.02.   The space plan must be approved in writing by both Landlord and Tenant, and preparation of the working drawings by Landlord's Architect shall not commence prior to such approval. Tenant, subject to the Architect's Allowance, shall pay the cost and expense of the preparation by Landlord's Architect of the working drawings.

    1.03.   If Tenant shall arrange for interior design services, whether with Landlord's space planner or with any other planner or designer, it shall be Tenant's responsibility and expense to

Client: _____ Runyan Management Services _____ Project: _____ p2j1 _____

cause necessary coordination of its planners' and designers' efforts with the efforts of the planners and designers of Landlord to insure that no delays are caused to either the planning or construction of the required Landlord's Work.

2.   Completion of Leased Premises.

(i) Any delay resulting from a failure by Tenant to approve or reasonably reject any shop drawings, samples, mock-ups, or models within five (5) days of submission thereof shall be charged to Tenant.

(ii) Tenant agrees to pay Landlord the total additional cost of all work to complete the Leasehold Improvements in excess of the prior approved plans and specifications, and Tenant agrees to pay Landlord an additional amount equal to fifteen percent (15%) of all such costs to cover the overhead costs of Landlord, within ten (10) days after being billed therefor.

2.01.   If there are any changes in Tenant's Work by or on behalf of Tenant from the work as reflected in the final working drawings, each such change must receive the prior written approval of Landlord and must be paid for by Tenant to the extent that the cost thereof exceeds the Cash Allowance.

2.02.   Under no circumstances whatsoever will Tenant or Tenant's authorized representative ever alter or modify or in any manner disturb any system or installation of the Building, including, but not limited to, central plumbing system, central electrical system, central heating, ventilating and air conditioning systems, central fire protection and fire alert systems, central building maintenance systems, central structural systems, elevators, and anything located within the central core of the Building.

2.03.   Tenant agrees that in the event of a default of payment under the Landlord's Contract, Tenant's Contract, or under this Work Letter Agreement, Landlord (in addition to all other remedies) has the same rights as in the event of default of payment of Rent under the Lease. Notwithstanding any provision contained herein to the contrary, it is understood and agreed that Landlord shall have no obligation to commence installation of any work in the Leased Premises until Tenant shall have caused to be furnished to Landlord and Landlord shall have approved the final working drawings as required by the provisions hereof. Notwithstanding the review and approval by Landlord of Tenant's plans and specifications, Landlord shall have no responsibility or liability in regard to the safety, sufficiency, adequacy, or legality of the Architect's plans and drawings or the Contractor's work, and Tenant shall be solely responsible for the compliance of such plans and specifications with all applicable laws and regulations, the architectural completeness and sufficiency thereof, the quality of work, and other matters relating thereto.

Business Technology Consultants
Project and Job Information

Client: Runyan Management Services Project: p2j1

RUNYAN MANAGEMENT SERVICES
A Massachusetts proprietary company

By: Managing Director

By: ____________________________

Title: ___________________________

AGREED AND ACCEPTED this **<insert day here>** day of **<insert month here>**, 200X

____

By: ________________________

Title: ______________________

Business Technology Consultants

• • • **Job Planning Form** • • •

Client: _____ Project:_____ Job: _____

1. What deliverables does the client expect for this job? (Examples include letter, printed report, slide presentation, database file, template, spreadsheet.)

2. Which additional resources, if any, do you need in finding information to complete the job? (Examples include Internet searches and documents on disk.)

3. What software do you need to complete this job?

4. What special software formatting features does the job call for?

STUDENT LOG

Name: _____ Date/Time Completed: _____

Document File Name(s): _____

Comments:

Client: Runyan Management Services   Project: p2j2

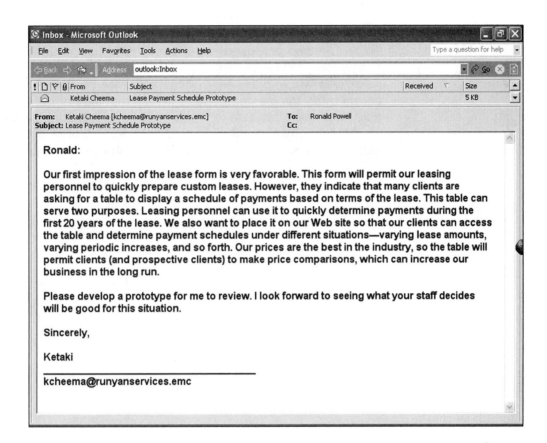

Inbox - Microsoft Outlook

File Edit View Favorites Tools Actions Help   Type a question for help

Back   Address outlook:Inbox   Go

! D ∇ 0 | From   Subject   Received ∇ | Size
          Ketaki Cheema   Lease Payment Schedule Prototype   5 KB

From: Ketaki Cheema [kcheema@runyanservices.emc]   **To:** Ronald Powell
Subject: Lease Payment Schedule Prototype   **Cc:**

Ronald:

Our first impression of the lease form is very favorable. This form will permit our leasing personnel to quickly prepare custom leases. However, they indicate that many clients are asking for a table to display a schedule of payments based on terms of the lease. This table can serve two purposes. Leasing personnel can use it to quickly determine payments during the first 20 years of the lease. We also want to place it on our Web site so that our clients can access the table and determine payment schedules under different situations—varying lease amounts, varying periodic increases, and so forth. Our prices are the best in the industry, so the table will permit clients (and prospective clients) to make price comparisons, which can increase our business in the long run.

Please develop a prototype for me to review. I look forward to seeing what your staff decides will be good for this situation.

Sincerely,

Ketaki

_____
kcheema@runyanservices.emc

Business Technology Consultants
Project and Job Information

Client: Runyan Management Services Project: p2j2

Job #2

NOTES

Files Needed
computer.bmp
book.bmp

At Ronald Powell's request, Tony Burdette considered the project Ketaki Cheema proposed and made several design and layout suggestions. When Ronald shared the recommendations with Ketaki, she was in agreement. She wants to see the final workbook design using sample data. She requested that the first two sets of data used to test the lease form design in the previous job be used for this purpose. She asked Ronald to provide a printed copy that displays each set of data. Below are the recommendations from Tony.

Client: _____ Runyan Management Services _____ Project: _____ p2j2 _____

Recommendations for the RMS Lease Schedule Project
Tony Burdette, Graphic Arts Design Specialist

1. A heading is needed that will indicate the name of the table and also create a good first impression. The heading should include a clip art image to make it more interesting. An abacus, book, or calculator are good possibilities to attract attention since these are traditional tools.

2. To build on the above idea, consider using a three-part heading. One part will be the heading text. Another part will be the traditional tool. A third part will be a modern computer. This idea builds on the comparison between the old and the new—it can mirror the rich RMS heritage while portraying the company to be in tune with the modern age.

3. Two images that you may want to consider for inclusion in the heading section are shown below. Some sizing may be needed so that the two images will be approximately equal in size on the payment schedule.

4. Since some users will be Web surfers, the table wording and layout must be clear and user-friendly. A prompt is needed to let them know what is needed and where it should be entered. Here is an example:

Enter the monthly installment amount and rate of increase below in order to create a payment schedule for your lease. Enter the rate of increase as a number, such as 7 to indicate 7 percent or 7.5 to indicate 7.5 percent.

Enter the monthly installment amount here:	
Enter the rate of increase here:	

Client: _____ Runyan Management Services _____ Project: _____ p2j2 _____

5. A payment schedule table, including appropriate formulas, should display so as to provide the needed information about the payments. A schedule similar to the one shown below (example covers the first three years) which is based on an installment amount during the first year and a six percent annual rate of increase, is recommended. Currency amounts should be rounded to zero decimal places. A cell bottom border can be used to provide lines where values will be entered. Of course, formulas will need to be placed on the schedule to make needed calculations.

Payment Number	Installment Amount	Annual Amount
1 to 12	$20,000	$240,000
13 to 24	$21,200	$254,400
25 to 36	$22,472	$269,664
∧∧∧∧∧∧∧	∧∧∧∧∧∧∧	∧∧∧∧∧∧∧∧

6. All of the leases at Runyan Management Services run for a minimum of 20 years, so calculations should cover a 20-year period—based on the two variables that are entered by the user.

7. With the appropriate use of WordArt and/or text boxes, a really attractive design can be created for this project. We may want to experiment with AutoFormat for the table, but custom fill, fonts, and color applications will make the table interesting and attractive. This is particularly important since the payment schedule computations will appear on the Web site. My recommendation is to try it both ways and then decide on the one with the better appearance.

Client: _____ Project:_____ Job: _____

1. What deliverables does the client expect for this job? (Examples include letter, printed report, slide presentation, database file, template, spreadsheet.)

2. Which additional resources, if any, do you need in finding information to complete the job? (Examples include Internet searches and documents on disk.)

3. What software do you need to complete this job?

4. What special software formatting features does the job call for?

STUDENT LOG

Name: _____ Date/Time Completed: _____

Document File Name(s): _____

Comments:

Client: _____Runyan Management Services_____ Project: _____p3j1_____

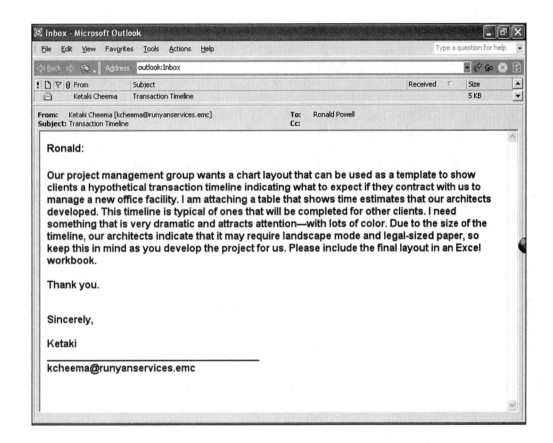

Business Technology Consultants
Project and Job Information

Client: **Runyan Management Services**   Project: **p3j1**

Job #1

Files Needed
timeline.doc
transaction.xls
btc_logo.jpg

Below is the table Ketaki Cheema attached to provide tasks and completion requirements that should be placed on the transaction timeline workbook form. She indicated that she needs the template as soon as possible so a client can make a decision about which management company to use for a proposed project. She requested that the July 1 date correspond to next year with the year designation for other dates adjusted accordingly.

Ronald Powell forwarded information about the job to Tony Burdette. Tony provided a set of recommendations along with a partial layout to serve as a foundation for the final design that will be presented to Ketaki. Materials from Tony are on the following pages.

Task Duration	Beginning Date	Task
1 month	July 1	Requirement definitions, process development, surveys
2 months	August 1	Full survey and analysis
1 month	September 15	Identify short list of preferred locations
2.5 months	September 1	Engage architect, develop specifications
1 month	October 15	Develop and issue request for proposal
1 month	November 15	Developers prepare proposals
1 month	December 15	Proposals received, analyzed, counterproposal developed
1 month	January 15	Counterproposal issued
2 weeks	February 15	Proposals received, location selected, final offer to developer
6 weeks	February 15	Lease negotiations and final pricing
10 months	April 1 to January of the following year	10 months of architectural and construction
1 month	February of the following year	Final tenant move-in and punch list

Client: _____ Runyan Management Services _____ Project: _____ p3j1 _____

Recommendations for the RMS Transaction Timeline Project
Tony Burdette, Graphic Arts Design Specialist

1. Our department developed the accompanying layout to meet the needs that were expressed by Ketaki Cheema. I have also developed a workbook form (in its early stages) that may be beneficial as you develop the final design for the document that will be presented to RMS. At least it shows how color can be used to match Ketaki's requirement to include lots of color. A different color fill for each month is recommended.

2. Placement of a logo, to appear on the left side of the company name, is recommended. Perhaps a clip art image showing an office building or office environment would be good.

3. The name of the company should be in the largest font on the document. WordArt can be used to enhance the company name.

4. The background that includes the task text will look sharp with a white fill and a black font.

5. Care must be taken to plot the timeline with the month so that the color fill relates to the time that the task is in progress by showing the period of time that it takes to complete. The text for the task begins to the right of the time period. This is depicted on the sample layout design.

6. A soft color should be used to fill the column containing project duration notations.

7. A rather neutral color, such as light gray, should be placed in the area from the project duration column to the point where the transaction time begins. This will provide contrast that will better highlight the color.

8. The color fill that is used for the month should be extended to include activities that will be completed during the month.

9. Include a notation (along with our company logo) indicating that our company developed the project, but show it as hidden text so that it will not display during the printing process. The notation should be placed below the bottom of the form.

10. Row heights will need to be adjusted to add emphasis. The design model will give you an idea about what our department thinks will be attractive.

Client: _____ Runyan Management Services _____ Project: ___ **p3j1** ___

Job #1

(continued)
Files Needed
timeline.doc
transaction.xls
btc_logo.jpg

Below is Tony's sample layout. Four events have been entered in the workbook so far to determine how the color schemes will appear and to get Ketaki's approval to continue with the project. Tony's suggested color formatting will also permit Ketaki to view a particular month and determine activities that are taking place during the month. The month of September is an example. It continues the "Full survey and analysis" that begins in August. "Identify short list of preferred locations" begins during the second half of September and continues until the middle of October. "Engage architect, develop specifications" begins on the first of September and continues until the middle of November.

A paper-size adjustment may be required so that the form will print on one page. In addition, the chart is needed in electronic form so that it can be attached to an e-mail message for Ketaki.

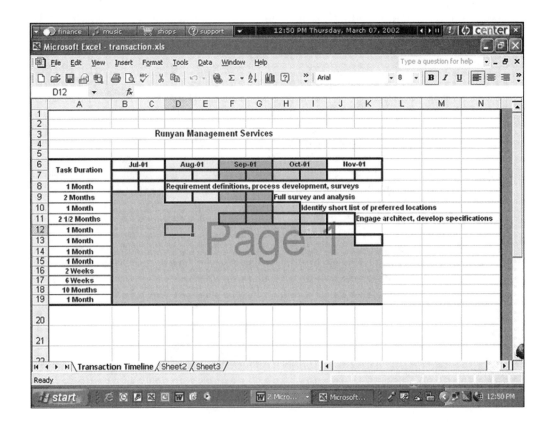

Business
Technology
Consultants

Client: _____ Project:_____ Job: _____

1. What deliverables does the client expect for this job? (Examples include letter, printed report, slide presentation, database file, template, spreadsheet.)

2. Which additional resources, if any, do you need in finding information to complete the job? (Examples include Internet searches and documents on disk.)

3. What software do you need to complete this job?

4. What special software formatting features does the job call for?

STUDENT LOG

Name: _____ Date/Time Completed: _____

Document File Name(s): _____

Comments:

Client: **Runyan Management Services**   Project: **p4j1**

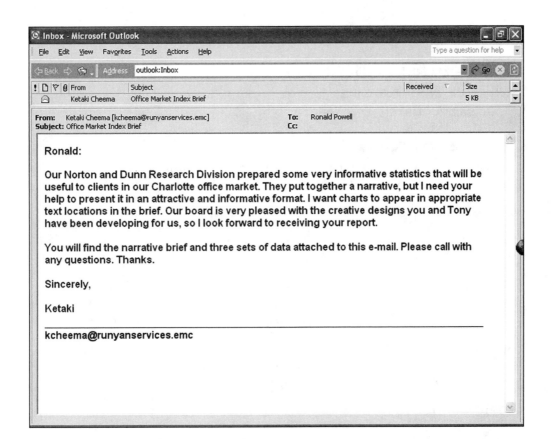

Job #1

Files Needed
office_survey.doc
occupancy.xls
absorption.xls
lease_rates.xls
office.gif

In a quick read-through of the brief, Ronald Powell noticed that the researchers placed the words "last year" instead of the actual year in the text, so it will be necessary to find and replace these words with the actual last year throughout the document. A phone call to Ketaki Cheema told Ronald that, while the data is not formatted or shown in chart form, it appears to be accurate. Ketaki requested that there be a border at the bottom of each page on the final report. She wants the footer to contain the following information: company name on the left, page number in the center, and the document title (Office Market Index) on the right side of the page. She also requested that a copy of the brief—text and charts—be provided for her review, along with a copy of the formatted workbook tables. Ronald asked Tony Burdette to review the brief and data and make suggestions for the design and layout of the report. Text for the brief, the sets of data, Tony's recommendations, and a planning form follow.

Client: _____ Runyan Management Services _____ Project: _____ p4j1 _____

OFFICE MARKET INDEX BRIEF
Charlotte, North Carolina
Third Quarter Report, Last Year

Market Overview

Over the first half of last year, national office supply grew by approximately 4%, according to Norton and Dunn Research, a division of Runyan Management Services. It is expected that over 75 million square feet of new office space will be delivered by the end of last year, with only 38% of that space preleased. Continuing the pattern that began during the first half of the year, vacancy rates are rising dramatically due to the addition of new buildings and sublease space to almost every major office market in the country. While the market experienced the same oversupply that has consumed the national market, there were signs of positive growth during the third quarter.

Positive net absorption of 37,743 square feet was recorded this quarter, and, while not dramatic, this was much higher than last quarter's negative absorption of -125,802 square feet. In spite of the over 400,000 square feet of sublease space available for lease, the demand for office space was still visible. New construction accounted for 147,200 square feet of space delivered this quarter, of which over 53% was preleased. Office development starts have come to a standstill as developers work to lease the product that is currently coming to the market. Three buildings were completed in the third quarter. Johnson Chemical-Mayberry Farms (104,000 sq. ft.), Darin Gate I (24,000 sq. ft.), and Darin Gate II (19,200 sq. ft.) were completed in the 485 Corridor, a submarket in which a large number of office developments have been delivered in the past two years. By year's end, this influential submarket will also see the delivery of 335,806 square feet. Other completions are expected in the East and Northeast submarkets by the end of the fourth quarter. Tower III at Sky Land Place in the East submarket will add 213,000 square feet of fully leased office space in the second quarter of next year.

OFFICE MARKET INDEX

OFFICE MARKET INDEX
Third Quarter, Last Year

Job Growth

Job growth in Mecklenburg County, recording the highest metropolitan unemployment rate in the state, registered at 3.9% as of September last year, down from 4.4% in June. Job growth in nonagricultural employment increased by 3,600 jobs, partially offset by losses in the industrial machinery/equipment industry. The state average unemployment rate registered at 4.0% in September, last year, down one-tenth of a percentage point from the previous month. However, fluctuations in unemployment rates continue to be seasonal in nature. The United States average

Client: _____Runyan Management Services_____ Project: ____p4j1____

unemployment rate for September, last year, remained at 4.9%, amid sharp job losses in manufacturing. National employment also fell in services, wholesale trade, and retail trade.
Source: Office of Labor Market Studies

OFFICE MARKET INDEX

OFFICE MARKET INDEX
Third Quarter, Last Year

Occupancy Rate
The overall occupancy rate was 85.9% at the end of the third quarter, last year, decreasing 0.5 percentage point from second quarter, last year, and 4.2 percentage points from third quarter of the previous year. While market-wide Class A occupancy increased to 88.4% from 87.8% at second quarter, last year, Class B occupancy decreased from 84.7% to 82.8% this quarter. The third quarter of last year reported a 91.8% occupancy rate for Class A properties and an 88.2% rate for Class B properties. Quarterly occupancy changes on a submarket level included the following: Airport (down from 86.2% to 85.4%), Downtown (up from 82.8% to 82.9%), East (up from 87.6% to 87.8%), 385 Corridor (down from 91.0% to 87.2%), Midtown (up from 82.0% to 86.0%), North (down from 84.3% to 82.7%), and Northeast (down from 82.5% to 79.8%).

Net Absorption
The office market experienced overall positive net absorption in the third quarter of last year, gaining 37,743 square feet from second quarter last year. Year-to-date absorption for the entire market totaled -119,752 square feet. For comparison, absorption totaled 374,120 square feet at third quarter, last year. Year-to-date absorption for Class A buildings was 196,984 square feet and for Class B buildings was -316,736 square feet. Third quarter absorption by submarket was as follows: East (up 18,247 sq. ft.), 385 Corridor (up 19,191 sq. ft.), Midtown (up 42,266 sq. ft.), Downtown (up 4,664 sq. ft.), Airport (down 13,575 sq. ft.), North (down 4,915 sq. ft.), and Northeast (down 28,135 sq. ft.). The largest absorption by submarket and class was East Class A properties, gaining 86,983 square feet this quarter.

Average Asking Lease Rates
The overall average asking lease rate dropped $0.04 from second quarter of last year to $17.04 per square foot this quarter. However, this was an increase of $0.11 over the asking lease rate of $16.93 recorded at third quarter of the previous year. Since last year, overall asking lease rates had moved steadily upward. Class A rates rose $0.09 to $18.88 per square foot, compared to the third quarter last year rate of $18.60 per square foot. Class B rates dropped $0.20 this quarter to $14.94 per square foot. East Class A lease rates rose $0.02, reaching $20.03 per square foot. Quarterly changes in lease rates were reported in the following submarkets: Airport (up $0.19 to $13.49), East (down $0.10 to $18.87), Downtown (up $0.06 to $15.57), Midtown (down $0.02 to $15.12), North (down $0.44 to $11.47), Northeast (down $0.11 to $15.18), and 385 Corridor (up $0.21 to $18.07).

Client: _____ Runyan Management Services _____ Project: _____ p4j1 _____

Occupancy Rate
Charlotte, North Carolina, Office Market

Area	First Quarter	Second Quarter	Third Quarter
Airport	95.1%	86.2%	85.4%
Downtown	83.1%	82.8%	82.9%
East	91.5%	87.6%	87.8%
385 Corridor	95.2%	91.0%	87.2%
Midtown	86.1%	82.0%	86.0%
North	80.9%	84.3%	82.7%
Northeast	85.0%	82.5%	79.8%
Overall	81.7%	80.9%	85.9%

Net Absorption
Charlotte, North Carolina, Office Market

Area	First Quarter	Second Quarter	Third Quarter
Airport	4,521	-48,375	-13,575
Downtown	151,525	75,253	4,664
East	100,115	-100,753	18,247
385 Corridor	55,621	-48,735	19,191
Midtown	1,003	4,217	42,266
North	2,121	1,815	-4,915
Northeast	46,532	-2,176	-28,135

Average Asking Lease Rates
Charlotte, North Carolina, Office Market

Area	First Quarter	Second Quarter	Third Quarter
Airport	$13.35	$13.30	$13.49
Downtown	$15.50	$15.51	$15.57
East	$18.89	$18.97	$18.87
385 Corridor	$17.72	$17.86	$18.07
Midtown	$14.75	$15.14	$15.12
North	$11.52	$11.91	$11.47
Northeast	$15.07	$15.29	$15.18
Overall	$16.93	$17.00	$17.04

Client: _____ Runyan Management Services _____ Project: _____ p4j1 _____

Recommendations from Tony Burdette

1. For each workbook, a bar chart is needed to show comparisons for each geographic section and for each quarter within the section—perhaps a subdivided bar chart. You will probably want to save the chart separately so that it can be easily inserted into the text document. Since space will be limited when you insert the charts into the report, you may want to abbreviate the geographic locations for chart labels. I recommend a vertical bar chart for each one with geographic labels across the x-axis and appropriate numerical values shown on the y-axis. The numerical scale for each chart will need to be adjusted to a reasonable and appropriate range.

2. Combining the three tables into one file will permit all of the data relating to the project to be located in one workbook, with sheets appropriately labeled. The tables in the present files are not formatted; they should be, to make them more attractive.

3. The document text relating to the three areas (Occupancy Rate, Net Absorption, and Average Asking Lease Rates) should be formatted so that the text appears on the left side of the page and the related chart appears on the right side of the page. This will keep the text and chart together in the document.

4. The text will have a more professional appearance if it is right-aligned. I recommend Arial font (size 11), but do experiment with font type and size options to get one that you feel RMS will like for the brief.

5. The office building clip art image should appear across the entire width of the top of the document. Adjust the main and sectional title font sizes to make them more attractive. A copy of the image is shown below.

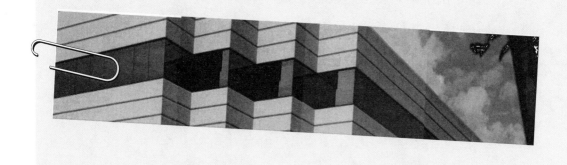

Client: _____Runyan Management Services_____ Project: _____p4j1_____

Planning Form

File	File Purpose and/or Notes
office_survey.doc	
occupancy.xls	
absorption.xls	
lease_rates.xls	
office.gif	

Business
Technology
Consultants

• • • Job Planning Form • • •

Client: _____ Project: _____ Job: _____

1. What deliverables does the client expect for this job? (Examples include letter, printed report, slide presentation, database file, template, spreadsheet.)

2. Which additional resources, if any, do you need in finding information to complete the job? (Examples include Internet searches and documents on disk.)

3. What software do you need to complete this job?

4. What special software formatting features does the job call for?

STUDENT LOG

Name: _____ Date/Time Completed: _____

Document File Name(s): _____

Comments:

Client: _____ Runyan Management Services _____ Project: _____ p5j1 _____

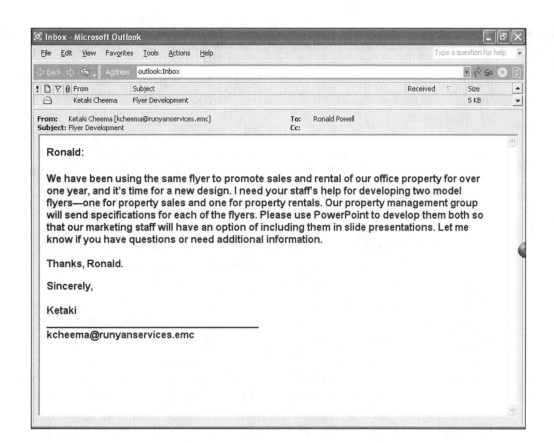

Inbox - Microsoft Outlook

File   Edit   View   Favorites   Tools   Actions   Help   Type a question for help

Back   Address   outlook:Inbox   Go

!	From	Subject	Received	Size
	Ketaki Cheema	Flyer Development		5 KB

From: Ketaki Cheema [kcheema@runyanservices.emc]   **To:** Ronald Powell
Subject: Flyer Development   **Cc:**

Ronald:

We have been using the same flyer to promote sales and rental of our office property for over one year, and it's time for a new design. I need your staff's help for developing two model flyers—one for property sales and one for property rentals. Our property management group will send specifications for each of the flyers. Please use PowerPoint to develop them both so that our marketing staff will have an option of including them in slide presentations. Let me know if you have questions or need additional information.

Thanks, Ronald.

Sincerely,

Ketaki

_____

kcheema@runyanservices.emc

Job #1

Files Needed
logo.gif
pinecrest.jpg
diagram.jpg
map.jpg

When Ronald Powell called Ketaki Cheema to discuss the flyers, she told him she wants a layout that includes both information and pictures depicting the property for sale or rental. She asked him to vary font color and size as well as fill colors to add interest to the design. She prefers an uncluttered design, yet wants all the space used wisely. Each flyer must fit on an 8½" × 11" sheet in a portrait orientation. The property management group from RMS sent project specifications for the Pine Crest sales property flyer. Ketaki indicated that the group's specifications should be followed; however, she gave BTC considerable flexibility for determining the layout and design as long as the flyer is attractive and functional. Tony Burdette reviewed the specifications and provided a form for planning the layout. These documents are on the next pages.

Business Technology Consultants
Project and Job Information

Client: Runyan Management Services   Project: p5j1

Flyer Specifications—Property for Sale
1. The company logo must appear across the entire top of the flyer with the company name, Runyan Management Services, added to the left portion of the logo and the words "Commitment and Service" added to the right portion of the logo with white font lettering.
2. The following notation should appear in larger-than-normal font size near the bottom edge of the logo: Office Building For Sale. The words "For Sale" should appear in a red font and be slightly larger than the words "Office Building," which should appear in a black font.
3. A picture of the office building should appear immediately after the above notation on the right side of the flyer. The picture should extend over approximately 60 percent of the width of the space allowed for the flyer. The following text should appear on top of the picture and on separate lines with a white font: 1935 York Street, Suite 216, St. Petersburg, FL 33578.
4. The following financial information should appear on two separate lines in an appropriate location: Square Feet: +/- 5,500 and Sale Price: $535,000.
5. A diagram should appear on the left side of the flyer.
6. A location map should appear on the left side of the flyer.
7. The following bulleted (red square bullet) items should appear in an area under the facility picture: Completely renovated in 2001; 3 Separate HVAC units including one 24-hour unit dedicated to separate telephone and server rooms; CAT-5 wiring throughout with 49 network connections; Upgraded finishes throughout including custom built receptionist desk, coffered ceiling, and built-in cubicles.
8. Include contact information on the bottom portion of the flyer as follows: Opal Gamble, (800) 555-4327, ogamble@bnet.emc.

Client: _____ Runyan Management Services _____ Project: _____ p5j1 _____

Sales Flyer Layout Sheet—Pine Crest

Items for the top portion of the flyer

**Items for the left portion of the flyer
(40 percent of the flyer width)**

**Items for the right portion of the flyer
(60 percent of the flyer width)**

Items for the bottom portion of the flyer

Business Technology Consultants

● ● ● **Job Planning Form** ● ● ●

Client: _____ Project: _____ Job: _____

1. What deliverables does the client expect for this job? (Examples include letter, printed report, slide presentation, database file, template, spreadsheet.)

2. Which additional resources, if any, do you need in finding information to complete the job? (Examples include Internet searches and documents on disk.)

3. What software do you need to complete this job?

4. What special software formatting features does the job call for?

STUDENT LOG

Name: _____ Date/Time Completed: _____

Document File Name(s): _____

Comments:

Client: _____Runyan Management Services_____ Project: _____p5j2_____

N O T E S

Job #2

Files Needed
logo.gif
arbor1.jpg
arbor2.jpg
arbor3.jpg

The property management group from Runyan Management Services sent project specifications for the flyer for the Arbor Plaza rental property. Ketaki Cheema reminded Ronald Powell that the general guidelines they discussed for the sales property flyer regarding color, appearance, size, and orientation applied to this flyer as well. Ronald again called on Tony Burdette to review the specifications (below) and provide a form (on the following page) for planning the Arbor Plaza flyer. Tony told Ronald to strive for a good balance in placing the items for the final layout.

Flyer Specifications—Property for Rent
1. The company logo must appear across the entire top of the flyer with the company name, Runyan Management Services, added to the left portion of the logo and the words "Commitment and Service" added to the right portion of the logo with white font lettering.
2. A picture, along with the name and address of the property, is needed for the flyer. The building name is Arbor Plaza. The address is 36 Arbor Court, Baltimore, Maryland. The picture and caption should appear on the right side of the flyer, beginning below the bottom edge of the logo.
3. Information about the facility should appear in a section below the picture and include the following information: Square Feet: 31,600 square feet per floor; Rental Rate: $17.00–$18.50 (Office), $16.15 (Retail). This financial information should be followed by nine customized bulleted items in a vertical design: Magnificent lobby; 24-hour on-duty security; Adjacent covered parking garage; Tenant-controlled heating and air conditioning; After-hours heating and air conditioning available; State-of-the-art fire alarm and sprinkler system; On-site management office; Personal office design and finish; Storage space available. All information in this section should appear in a blue font on a white fill color background.
4. A picture showing the inside of the building is needed with the following caption above the picture: The Mainstream of Baltimore Commerce. A dark background fill color, with a white font, is desired for this section.
5. A picture showing the outside of the building is needed with the following caption shown below the picture: Major tenants include: Barton Smith, PLLC; Syed, Jones, & Taylor; and Fults and Perez. A dark background fill, with white font, is desired for this section.
6. The name and phone number of the listing agent should be included on the flyer: Nancy Kratzy, (800) 555-2056.
7. A customized banner should be placed near the bottom of the flyer. An Internet site should be helpful for locating and developing a banner as long as copyright laws are followed.

Client: Runyan Management Services   Project: p5j2

Rental Flyer Layout Sheet—Arbor Plaza

Items for the top portion of the flyer

Items for the left portion of the flyer

Items for the right portion of the flyer

Items for the bottom portion of the flyer

Business Technology Consultants

· · · **Job Planning Form** · · ·

Client: _____ Project: _____ Job: _____

1. What deliverables does the client expect for this job? (Examples include letter, printed report, slide presentation, database file, template, spreadsheet.)

2. Which additional resources, if any, do you need in finding information to complete the job? (Examples include Internet searches and documents on disk.)

3. What software do you need to complete this job?

4. What special software formatting features does the job call for?

STUDENT LOG

Name: _____ Date/Time Completed: _____

Document File Name(s): _____

Comments:

Client: _____Runyan Management Services_____ Project: _____p6j1_____

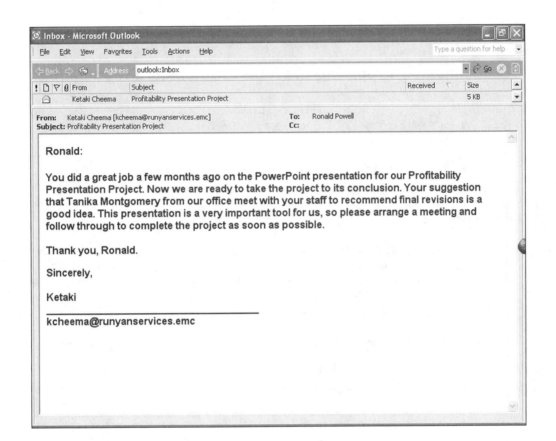

Job #1

Files Needed
profitability.ppt
rmsmovie.swf

Ronald Powell reviewed the presentation with Tanika Montgomery and Tony Burdette. Following their meeting, Tony and Tanika consulted with Ketaki Cheema about a number of specifics and then prepared a detailed set of recommendations for finalizing the presentation. Tony also provided a separate guide for inserting a Flash movie into a blank PowerPoint slide. The guidelines begin on the next page. Ketaki requested that someone at BTC view the presentation when it is finished, to make sure that everything is working properly. She wants a printed copy of the slide show (six slides per page) along with the file on disk.

Client: _____ Runyan Management Services _____ Project: _____ p6j1 _____

Guidelines for Preparing the RMS Profitability Presentation

TITLE SLIDE

The title slide ("Asset Services") appears to be out of order. This slide should be moved to the beginning of the presentation.

PROPERTY MANAGEMENT SLIDE

The slide titled "Property Management" needs something to make it more attractive. A clip art image depicting an office building is recommended for the upper-right corner of the form. The Internet can be used to locate and download an appropriate image.

CALCULATION OF ACCOUNTING POINTS SLIDE

Ketaki requested that formulas be added to the slide titled "Calculation of Accounting Points" so that she can show a completed form as part of the presentation. A review of the workbook format that was used to create the form revealed that the following computations are needed. In addition, change the fill color to light yellow for each cell that currently has a gray shade.

Cell Address	Action Needed
F6	Multiply cell F4 by cell E6.
F7	Multiply cell F4 by cell E7.
B13	Multiply cell B10 by cell B11.
C17	Multiply the Indirect Overhead amount by the Columbia Accounting percent.
C18	Repeat the above process for the Charleston indirect overhead computation.
C19	Repeat the above process for the Corporate indirect overhead computation.
B26	Reference the contents of cell F6—same value as cell F6.
B27	Reference the contents of cell C17—same value as cell C17.
C26	Reference the contents of cell F7—same value as cell F7.
C27	Reference the contents of cell C18—same value as cell C18.
D26	Enter the following formula: =+(73000 * 1.0765) * 1.04 + 4200 + 75 − 5000
D27	Reference the contents of cell C19—same value as cell C19.
B29–D29	Enter an appropriate formula to compute the total for each area.
B36	Multiply cell B34 by the value 11.
C36	Multiply cell C34 by the value 11.

Client: _____ Runyan Management Services _____ Project: _____ p6j1 _____

MASTER SLIDE AND FOOTER

The master slide can be revised so that the company name, Runyan Management Services, appears at the bottom (center) of each slide. A footer can be added so that the current date appears at the bottom (left side) of each slide.

FEE PRICING ALLOCATIONS SLIDE

Ketaki requested that a slide be added to the presentation to follow the second slide that is titled "Objective." The slide will be used to show fee pricing allocation percents for corporate indirect costs. This is a very important slide, so color and layout should be used to make it appear as attractive as possible. Recommendations for this slide are as follows:

- The title, "Fee Pricing Allocations," should be shown in a large white font.
- The subtitle, "Corporate Indirect Costs," should be shown in a slightly smaller bright-red font.
- Each of the three charts should be included on this same slide. The chart for Asset Services should appear on the left, the chart for Brokerage Services should appear in the middle, and the chart for Accounting Services should appear on the right side of the slide, below the subtitle.
- Charts should be sized and placed in positions so that a small amount of space appears between each chart.
- Use fill and font colors as needed to make an attractive design.
- Show percents in the chart. Do not show leader lines. Place the legend at the bottom of each chart. A sample suggested format including a recommended color scheme for each of the charts on the slide is shown below, followed by a suggested layout for the "Fee Pricing Allocations" slide and the data for preparing the charts.

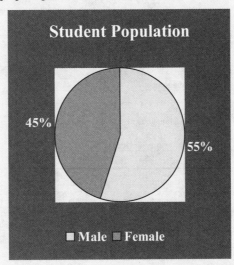

Client: ___Runyan Management Services___ Project: ___p6j1___

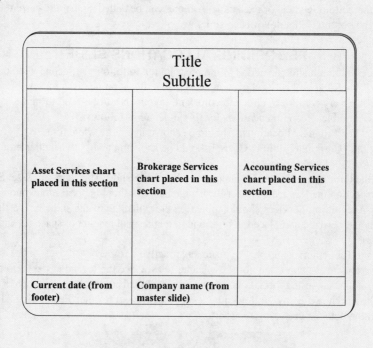

Recommended Design Layout for the "Fee Pricing Allocations" Slide

Data for Asset Services (Chart 1)

Asset Services	
Property Management	$241,716
Leasing	$241,615
Strategic Clients	$85,540
Construction Management	$85,325

Data for Brokerage Services (Chart 2)

Brokerage Services	
Industrial Brokerage	$232,180
Investment Properties	$305,500
Office Tenants	$586,560
Corporate Services	$97,760

Data for Accounting Services (Chart 3)

Accounting Services	
Columbia	$29,328
Charleston	$58,656
Corporate	$9,776

Client: _____ Runyan Management Services _____ Project: _____ p6j1 _____

MULTIMEDIA SLIDE

Ketaki requested that a multimedia slide be added to the presentation as a final slide in the series. BTC's multimedia specialists prepared a multimedia presentation using Macromedia Flash to serve as the last slide in the presentation. Attached is a set of instructions that can be used to insert the Flash movie (multimedia) into the final slide.

Client: _____Runyan Management Services_____ Project: _____p6j1_____

EMBEDDING A FLASH MOVIE IN POWERPOINT

1. Insert a new, blank slide at the end of the presentation. This slide will play a Macromedia Flash movie (Shockwave Flash Object).
2. Click on View, Toolbars, and check the Control Toolbox option. Click on the last button in the Control Toolbox to select More Controls.
3. From the pull-down list of available controls, select Shockwave Flash Object.
4. Use the mouse to draw a box on the slide the size you would like for the movie screen to appear. (NOTE: Do not make the box so large that the entire slide is covered.)
5. Right-click on the box with the large X and select Properties from the pop-up menu. Under the Alphabetic tab, click on (Custom) and the **... button.**
6. The Property Pages dialog box should appear. Make the following entries assuming d:\ identifies the CD-ROM drive and rmsmovie.swf is the movie. Verify that only the following three options are checked: Play, Show Menu, and Embed Movie.

Movie URL	d:\rmsmovie.swf	
Base URL:	☑ Play	☐ Loop
Quality	Best	☐ Device Font	☑ Show Menu
Scale	ShowAll	☑ Embed Movie	
Align		Background Color
Window Mode	Window	

7. Click OK to finish embedding the movie (do not click Apply).
8. Under the Properties window, verify that the Playing option is set to True. Close the Properties window, and the Flash movie is ready to play.
9. Press F5 or select Slide Show and View Show to test the entire presentation for accuracy. The final slide should play the Flash movie.

HELPFUL HINTS FOR FLASH MOVIES:

1. Match the movie background to the background of your PowerPoint presentation.
2. If the Flash movie does not play, open the Properties window again and check the Playing property. If it is set to False, click Playing and the down arrow to change the Playing property to True.
3. While the movie is playing, right-click to access the Controls menu for functions such as rewinding or pausing the movie.
4. PowerPoint cannot recognize mouse clicks on top of a Flash object, so do not make the Flash object the full size of the slide. You will need to leave an area in order to click away from the movie.
5. If a Flash movie includes Internet hyperlinks, these links will continue to function in PowerPoint.

● ● ● **Job Planning Form** ● ● ●

Client: _____ Project: _____ Job: _____

1. What deliverables does the client expect for this job? (Examples include letter, printed report, slide presentation, database file, template, spreadsheet.)

2. Which additional resources, if any, do you need in finding information to complete the job? (Examples include Internet searches and documents on disk.)

3. What software do you need to complete this job?

4. What special software formatting features does the job call for?

STUDENT LOG

Name: _____ Date/Time Completed: _____

Document File Name(s): _____

Comments:

Client: _____ Runyan Management Services _____ Project: _____ p7j1 _____

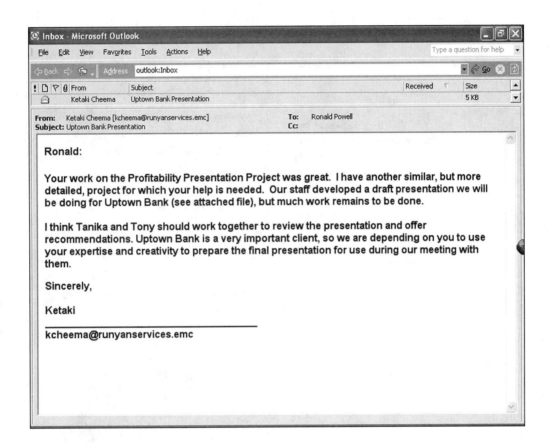

Job #1

Files Needed
uptown.ppt
runyan_logo.gif
uptown.jpg

Tanika Montgomery and Tony Burdette reviewed and corrected the presentation before making recommendations. The slides begin on the next page and are followed by the preparation guidelines. As with the preceding Profitability presentation, Ketaki Cheema wants a printed copy of the slide show (six slides per page) along with the file on disk.

Client: **Runyan Management Services**   Project: **p7j1**

PROPOSAL FOR
COMPREHENSIVE REAL ESTATE SERVICES
PRESENTED TO
Uptown Bank

Presented by
Runyan Management Services

Summary of RMS Benefits

Transition Team Commitment

Reduced FM Expenses $10,000,000

Increased Customer Satisfaction 10%

Financial Industry Experience

Global Service Delivery Group

Local Oversight/Regional Support Structure

Separate FM Division

Market Environment

Corporate Real Estate Outsourcing

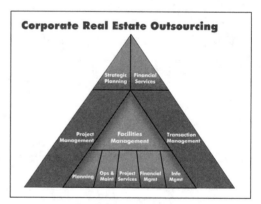

Strategic Planning · Financial Services · Project Management · Facilities Management · Transaction Management · Planning · Ops & Maint · Project Services · Financial Mgmt · Info Mgmt

Corporate Outsource Opportunity

10% have outsourced facility management & real estate

67% have outsourced a major corporate function

Occupancy expenses equivalent to 15-20% net income

FM outsourcing reduces operating expenses by 15-25%

Uptown Bank Current Situation

34th largest bank holding company in U.S.

7.3 MSF in 853 offices and 1,218 ATMs in 15 states

Operational Strategy: consolidate and streamline operations to improve efficiency, customer service, and cost savings.

Client: Runyan Management Services   Project: p7j1

Runyan Management Services Projected Savings/Customer Service Enhancements For Uptown Bank

---

Projected Facility Management Savings

Assumptions - (1) $98 million net occupancy expenses
(2) 9.4 million square feet of space

	Low	High
Restack Office	$1,372,300	$3,084,600
Energy Mgmt.	2,038,500	4,077,000
Vendor Consolidation	1,243,100	2,852,900
Mtnc. Contractors	1,080,160	2,140,320
Purchasing	621,580	1,538,970
Total	$6,355,640	$13,693,790

Communicating Results: Example Impact On Stock Value Of Uptown Bank

Annual Reduction in Occupancy Cost	$10,000,000
÷ Shares Outstanding	138,487,000
Increased Earnings/Share	$0.072
Savings per Share	$0.072
x PE Ratio	12
Increase/Share	$0.864
Increase per Share	$0.864
x Shares Outstanding	138,487,000
Increased Shareholder Value	$119,652,768

Staffing Matrix – Uptown Bank

	# Sites	SF
Senior Facility Managers	150 – 200	1,750,000
Facility Managers	40 – 60	450,000
Technicians (route)	15 – 20	110,000
Technicians (admin)	1	150,000
Technicians (data/ops)	1	125,000

CSR   75 calls per day
A/P Clerk   1,300 invoices per month

Self-Performance Model – Uptown Bank

Criteria
- Technical Nature of Work
- Frequency of Use
- Risk Profile

Model

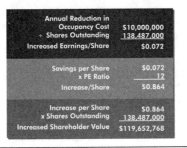

Service Level	Self Performance	Examples	Model Performed By:
Upper Tier	Highly Technical High Wage Rate Certifications Required	Annual PMIs Major Equipment Replacements	Alliance Partners Infrequent Utilization
Middle Tier	Highly Visible to Client Multi-skilled	Aesthetic Repairs / Tech Troubleshoot	RMS Technicians Increase Service Levels and Reduce Expenses
Lower Tier	Low Tech Low Wages	Janitorial Landscaping	Alliance Partners Labor Issues

---

Centralized Help Desk – Uptown Bank

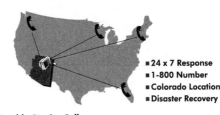

- 24 x 7 Response
- 1-800 Number
- Colorado Location
- Disaster Recovery

Monthly Service Calls
National Bank   12,000
Denver Mutual   7,500

Client: _____Runyan Management Services_____ Project: _____p7j1_____

Information Technology Strategy

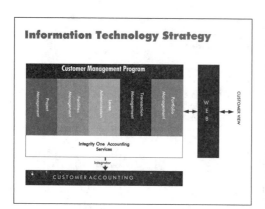

Customer Satisfaction

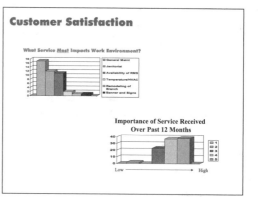

Case Studies

Southern Regional Bank

9.0 Million Sq. Ft. Portfolio
880 locations

COST SAVINGS
- $5M annual savings
- 10% on tools & materials
- 25% on lighting-related supplies
- 5% in annual utility costs
- 15% through self performance, negotiations & competitive pricing

ESTABLISHED CENTRALIZED CUSTOMER SERVICE DESK
- RMS has been tracking and reporting on various performance measures such as generated work orders and work order productivity, which improved by 10% during the first year.

Completed Conversion of First American Portfolio
- Completed sign conversion and transfer of 350 facilities to the Runyan Management Services portfolio.

First National Bank
23 Million Sq. Ft. Portfolio
2500 sites

SCOPE OF SERVICES
- Facilities Management
- Project Management
- Call Center
- Transaction Management
- Lease Administration

REDUCED OPERATING EXPENSES
- Within first 60 days reduced operating costs by $4 million, a 19% savings
- Headcount was reduced by 20%
- Standardized guidelines and procedures to provide consistency in operations

ESTABLISHED CENTRALIZED CUSTOMER SERVICE DESK
- 10,000 calls handled monthly

Western State Bank
17 Million Sq. Ft. Portfolio
1250 sites

SCOPE OF SERVICES
- Facility Management
- Project Management
- Transaction Management
- Lease Administration
- Systems Integration
- Customer Service

REDUCED OPERATING EXPENSES
- $1.3M in savings and $300K in collected receivables
- Energy management programs = savings of $.75 per sq. ft.

ESTABLISHED CENTRALIZED CUSTOMER SERVICE DESK
- 24-hour/7-day "800" hotline handles 12,000 calls monthly

Client: _____ Runyan Management Services _____ Project: _____ p7j1 _____

GUIDELINES FOR PREPARING
THE RMS UPTOWN BANK PRESENTATION

GENERAL RECOMMENDATIONS

(1) A design template is needed to add continuity to the presentation and make it more attractive. (2) Ketaki also wants BTC to rehearse the presentation and then set timings based on our best estimate about how much discussion time will be required for presenting each slide to executives at Uptown Bank. RMS will then make adjustments, if needed.

TITLE SLIDE

Ketaki sent a clip art image of the bank that she wants inserted at the top margin of the title slide. Make sure that the text will be fully visible on the slide after the clip art image is inserted.

CUSTOMIZED BULLET LISTING

Customized bullets are needed for the following slides to make them more attractive: "Summary of RMS Benefits" and "Corporate Outsource Opportunity."

SLIDE REMOVAL

Ketaki requested that the following slide be removed from the presentation: "Uptown Bank Current Situation."

TEXT LOCATION ADJUSTMENT

Adjust text for the slide titled "Runyan Management Services Projected Savings/Customer Service Enhancements For Uptown Bank" so that the text is centered vertically and horizontally on the slide.

SLIDE ADDITION

Ketaki needs a slide to follow the "Summary of RMS Benefits" slide to show the proposed organizational structure for the Uptown Bank/RMS Executive Team. She sent the following rough illustration to use to develop the organizational diagram and requested that (1) shadows be applied to each block in the diagram; (2) a white font be used for all letters except the title; (3) a different fill color be used for each block with the exception that Uptown Bank and SINGLE POINT OF ACCOUNTABILITY are to be prepared with the same fill color; (4) the title Uptown Bank/RMS Executive Team (green font) be entered for the diagram; and (5) bullets be added to the item list for the bottom block titled Service Delivery.

Client: _____ Runyan Management Services _____ Project: _____ p7j1 _____

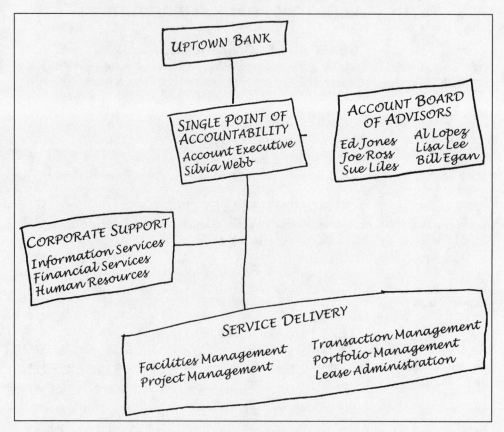

Uptown Bank/RMS Executive Team (draft for slide)

SLIDE ADDITION

Ketaki requested an additional slide to appear after the slide titled "Communicating Results: Example Impact On Stock Value Of Uptown Bank." She sent the rough draft copy shown below. Recommendations are that a light blue (or similar color) fill and bold white font be used for the box containing the revenue figures. Another recommendation is that the same fill color that is used for the above box be used for the title font.

Client: _____ Runyan Management Services _____ Project: _____ p7j1 _____

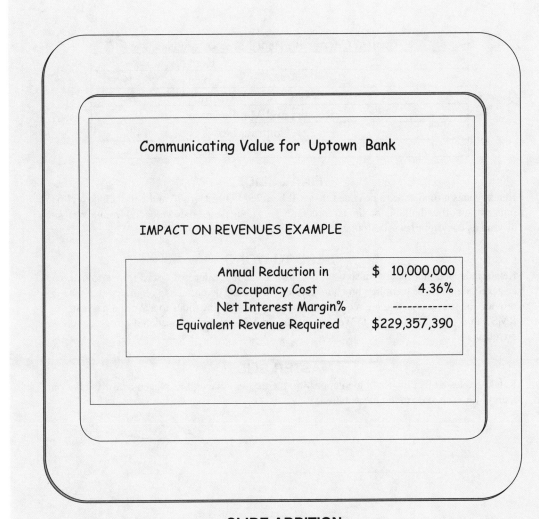

Communicating Value for Uptown Bank

IMPACT ON REVENUES EXAMPLE

Annual Reduction in	$ 10,000,000
Occupancy Cost	4.36%
Net Interest Margin%	------------
Equivalent Revenue Required	$229,357,390

SLIDE ADDITION

An additional slide was requested to appear after the slide titled "Corporate Outsource Opportunity" in the presentation. The chart will be used to show percents that relate to various real estate expenses. A 3D chart is needed, with the largest slice of the pie exploded to add emphasis to this expense. RMS sent the following data.

Client: _____Runyan Management Services_____ Project: _____p7j1_____

Typical Corporate Real Estate Expenses	
Rent	41%
Taxes	8%
Utilities	12%
Repairs and Maintenance	9%
Contract Services	11%
Depreciation	19%

FINAL SLIDE

Ketaki wants a final slide to be added that will be titled **"Questions?"** and will include a clip art image of an office building or similar structure. This image can be downloaded from a Web site as long as copyright laws are followed.

SEND TO WORD

Ketaki indicated that she may also want the slides to be in a Microsoft Word format to make it easier to use some of them in a brochure created in Word. Therefore, she requested that we provide the procedures that are required to send the PowerPoint slides to a Word document. RMS can perform the transfer to Word at the time that the slides are needed if our procedures are clear.

MASTER SLIDE

Ketaki requested that the RMS logo appear on the master slide and be placed below the bottom margin for each slide in the presentation.

Business
Technology
Consultants

Client: _____ Project: _____ Job: _____

1. What deliverables does the client expect for this job? (Examples include letter, printed report, slide presentation, database file, template, spreadsheet.)

2. Which additional resources, if any, do you need in finding information to complete the job? (Examples include Internet searches and documents on disk.)

3. What software do you need to complete this job?

4. What special software formatting features does the job call for?

STUDENT LOG

Name: _____ Date/Time Completed: _____

Document File Name(s): _____

Comments:

Client: _____Runyan Management Services_____ Project: _____p8j1_____

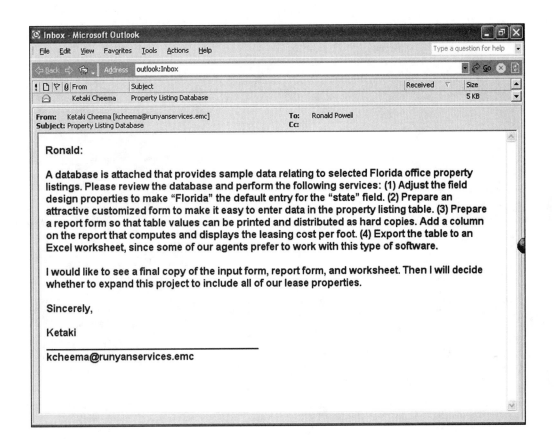

Job #1

Files Needed
listing.mdb
listing.xls

On the next two pages are screen captures showing the Access table, property listing, and data from Ketaki Cheema. Ronald Powell's staff provided forms that will be helpful while developing the formula to compute the lease cost per square foot and deciding on procedures for exporting the database to the worksheet.

Client: _____ Runyan Management Services _____ Project: _____ p8j1 _____

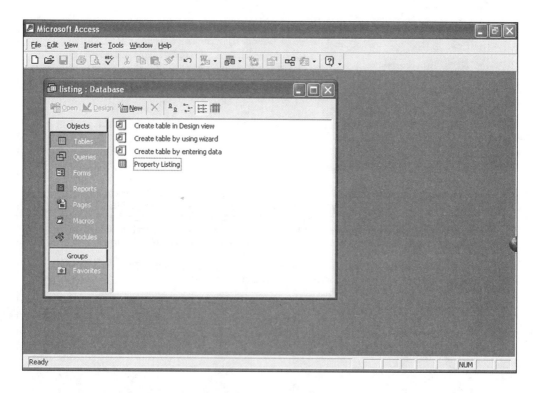

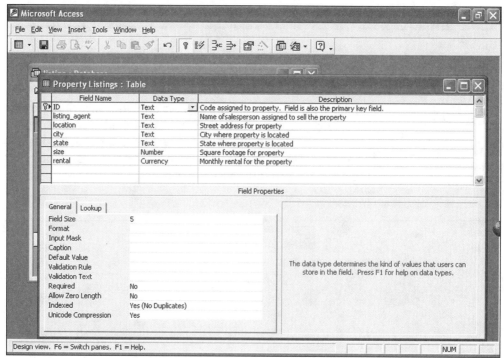

Client: Runyan Management Services   Project: p8j1

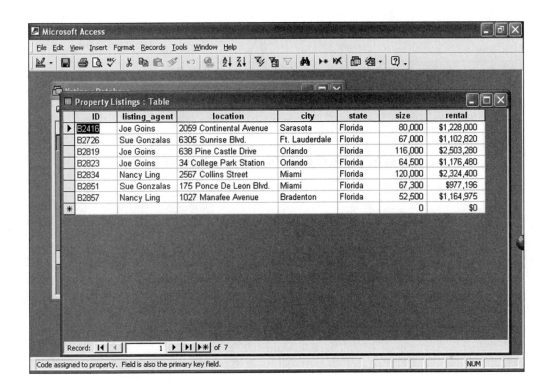

ID	listing_agent	location	city	state	size	rental
B2416	Joe Goins	2059 Continental Avenue	Sarasota	Florida	80,000	$1,228,000
B2726	Sue Gonzalas	6305 Sunrise Blvd.	Ft. Lauderdale	Florida	67,000	$1,102,820
B2819	Joe Goins	638 Pine Castle Drive	Orlando	Florida	116,000	$2,503,280
B2823	Joe Goins	34 College Park Station	Orlando	Florida	64,500	$1,176,480
B2834	Nancy Ling	2567 Collins Street	Miami	Florida	120,000	$2,324,400
B2851	Sue Gonzalas	175 Ponce De Leon Blvd.	Miami	Florida	67,300	$977,196
B2857	Nancy Ling	1027 Manafee Avenue	Bradenton	Florida	52,500	$1,164,975
*					0	$0

Record: 1 of 7

Code assigned to property. Field is also the primary key field.

Client: _____ Runyan Management Services _____ Project: _____ p8j1 _____

Verification of Formula and Results	
Formula	**Results**

Steps Needed to Export a Database to a Workbook File	
1.	
2.	
3.	
4.	
5.	

Job Planning Form

Client: _____ Project:_____ Job: _____

1. What deliverables does the client expect for this job? (Examples include letter, printed report, slide presentation, database file, template, spreadsheet.)

2. Which additional resources, if any, do you need in finding information to complete the job? (Examples include Internet searches and documents on disk.)

3. What software do you need to complete this job?

4. What special software formatting features does the job call for?

STUDENT LOG

Name: _____ Date/Time Completed: _____

Document File Name(s): _____

Comments:

CLIENT 5 First South Bank
Projects Overview

First South Bank (FSB), headquartered in New Orleans, is a diversified financial institution that offers services to member banks. It also provides financial products and services to over 510,000 retail and consumer customers. The bank is very proud that it has one of the best customer retention rates in the country. Investments and consumer finance are large service areas that include a full line of products such as mortgage loans, notes, and other lending programs; Internet banking; and insurance programs. FSB also offers standard and platinum credit cards plus a travel credit card for customers maintaining checking and credit balances above $10,000. In addition, the bank offers an ATM network that serves customers in twelve states. State-of-the-art technology is used for banking and transaction processing. The bank also distributes and underwrites fixed income and government agency securities.

The vision of FSB is to provide customers with the highest-quality products and services while operating in the most economical and efficient way possible. The corporate goal is to build a strong customer base by creating value for customers and developing solid loyalty ties to both customers and business partners. FSB's motto is: "Building our business one customer at a time." Over the past decade, this approach has permitted First South Bank to grow at a rate that is 25 percent higher than the industry average. Along with developing its customer base, FSB is committed to building and maintaining a staff that is the best in the banking industry.

Services Requested

First South Bank considers Business Technology Consultants (BTC) to be a very important partner in many activities that require a quick turnaround or specialized expertise in areas relating to Microsoft® Office applications. The bank has a constant need for computational and design layouts and has found that many of these specialized functions can be outsourced to BTC so that normal workflow is maintained efficiently. Brandon Dustin, director of external programs and

outsourcing, coordinates activities with Ronald Powell at BTC. Ronald is presently coordinating 11 projects for FSB, each consisting of a single job. An eleventh project has arrived on his desk as a result of his work with the bank and other clients. The projects are as follows:

- **Project 1** is the development of a Web page with links to banking agencies associated with the Department of Banking.

- **Project 2** involves creating an interest-computation table for the FSB Web site that customers can use to compare loan payments and interest savings when making regular payments versus a single end-of-loan-period payment.

- **Project 3** calls for the creation of a template for computing employee salary increases.

- **Project 4** requires editing a set of procedures for employees to follow when using an upgraded e-mail system and formatting the guidelines for placement on FSB's intranet.

- **Project 5** involves developing a workbook that bank customers can use on the Web to calculate a schedule of loan payments for various types of loans.

- **Project 6** relates to a workbook template FSB's field employees can use, via wireless devices, to compute maturity dates and values for securities.

- **Project 7** involves researching ways to access live financial data on the Internet and creating a tutorial that explains the process.

- **Project 8** calls for the development of a prototype for budgeting using the Excel goal-seeking function.

- **Project 9** requires adapting text and turning it into a three-panel, two-sided brochure for distribution to customers.

- **Project 10** focuses on the completion of an Excel worksheet for calculating bond maturity dates to be imported into Access as a database table.

- **Project 11** involves creating a résumé using a Web-based résumé wizard.

Client: _____ First South Bank _____ Project: _____ p1j1 _____

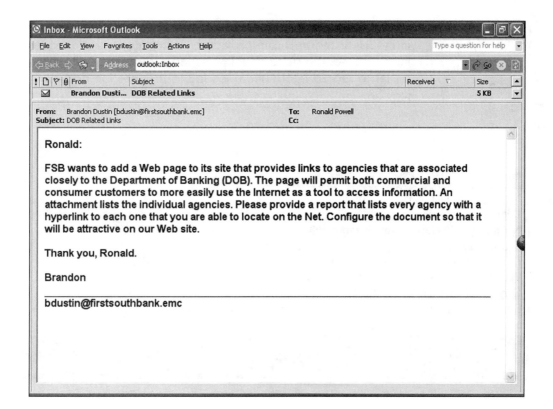

Client: _____ First South Bank _____ Project: _____ p1j1 _____

Job #1

NOTES

Files Needed
None

Use Internet search engines to locate Web sites for the agencies in the list Brandon Dustin provided. At Ronald Powell's request, the BTC research department provided a form that will make it easier to record information needed to prepare the document for FSB.

Department of Banking-Related Agencies
National Information Center (NIC)
Department of Treasury
National Credit Union Administration (NCUA)
Federal Financial Institutions Examination Council (FFIEC)
Federal Deposit Insurance Corporation (FDIC)
Federal Trade Commission (FTC)
Office of the Comptroller of the Currency (OCC)
Board of Governors of the Federal Reserve System (FRB)

Department of Banking-Related Agencies	
Agency	**Hyperlink**

Job Planning Form

Client: _____ Project: _____ Job: _____

1. What deliverables does the client expect for this job? (Examples include letter, printed report, slide presentation, database file, template, spreadsheet.)

2. Which additional resources, if any, do you need in finding information to complete the job? (Examples include Internet searches and documents on disk.)

3. What software do you need to complete this job?

4. What special software formatting features does the job call for?

STUDENT LOG

Name: _____ Date/Time Completed: _____

Document File Name(s): _____

Comments:

Client: _____ First South Bank _____ Project: _____ p2j1 _____

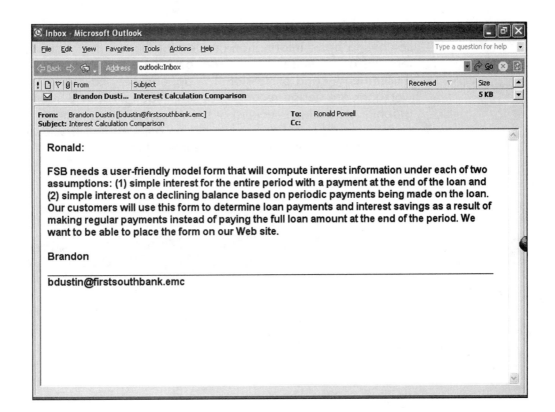

Business Technology Consultants
Project and Job Information

Client: _____ First South Bank _____ Project: _____ p2j1 _____

Job #1

Files Needed
interest.xls

Brandon Dustin sent Ronald Powell the following workbook containing basic information needed for the form. Of course, formulas and a more attractive design will be required to make it user-friendly and professional in appearance. Following the workbook are design recommendations made by Tony Burdette, graphic arts design specialist at BTC. Use the form on the next page to record formulas for determining amounts that should be computed to complete the Web site interest form.

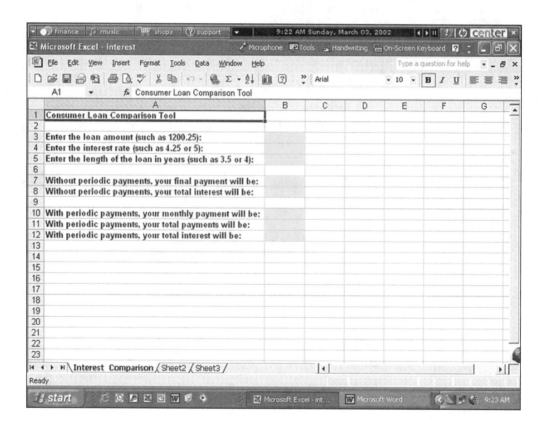

Client: _____ First South Bank _____ Project: _____ p2j1 _____

Consumer Loan Comparison Tool Recommendations

- Fonts should be larger throughout the form.

- Use fill and font color to make the form more attractive. Colors should match the existing Web site.

- Align text so that the text lines are closer to the amounts.

- Add fill color to serve as a divider for each section of the form.

- Print gridlines to provide more definition for columns.

- Add a cell border (bottom border) for each cell where a value is to be entered by the user.

- Format all values appropriately.

- Experiment with fill and font colors until the best combination is found to work on the Web site.

Interest Comparison Form—Formulas Needed	
Cell Address	**Formula**
B7	
B8	
B10	
B11	
B12	

Client:_____First South Bank_____ Project: _____p2j1_____

Job #1

(continued)
Files Needed
interest.xls

Brandon sent the following scenario for BTC to use in testing the interest form to verify that formulas are working properly. Use the "Values Obtained" form below and fill in the correct amounts.

Scenario

A bank customer borrows $27,500 to purchase an automobile with an intention to repay the amount within a three-year period. The interest rate for the loan is 8.5 percent. The customer wants to know the monthly payment that will be needed to pay for the automobile assuming that the full amount is financed. The customer also wants to know the total amount of interest and total amount paid under each of the following conditions: (1) the full loan amount, plus simple interest, is paid at the end of three years or (2) monthly payments are made so that the loan will be repaid within a three-year period.

Values Obtained

(a) The full amount needed to repay the loan at the end of three years without periodic payments will be:

_____

(b) If periodic payments are made, the amount of the monthly payment will be:

_____

(c) The total amount paid over the three-year period if periodic payments are made:

_____

Job #1

(continued)
Files Needed
interest.xls

Brandon also sent the solutions (shown in the box below) for verifying that the formulas are correctly entered. He then requested that the data be changed as follows: loan amount, $32,500; interest rate, 6.25 percent; time, 4 years. He also requested a printed copy of the completed interest form with this data entered to test the form.

(a) **$34,512.50**   (b) **$868.11**   (c) **$31,251.86**

Business Technology Consultants

Client: _____ Project:_____ Job: _____

1. What deliverables does the client expect for this job? (Examples include letter, printed report, slide presentation, database file, template, spreadsheet.)

2. Which additional resources, if any, do you need in finding information to complete the job? (Examples include Internet searches and documents on disk.)

3. What software do you need to complete this job?

4. What special software formatting features does the job call for?

STUDENT LOG

Name: _____ Date/Time Completed: _____

Document File Name(s): _____

Comments:

Client: **First South Bank**   Project: **p3j1**

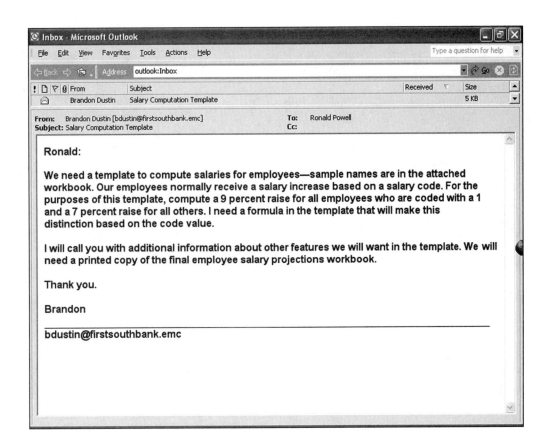

Job #1

Files Needed
salary.xls

Brandon Dustin called later and told Ronald Powell that he wants two additional columns: the raise amount and the proposed salary amount after the raise. He also wants formulas added that will compute the total, average, largest, and smallest amount for the current salary, raise, and proposed salary columns. Finally, he wants a comment added to the title cell indicating that this workbook is a salary computation draft template. A copy of the workbook that Brandon attached to his message is shown on the next page, along with recommendations for the workbook made by Tony Burdette. Following these documents are additional adjustments Brandon requested for the workbook along with a form for recording the necessary formulas.

Client: **First South Bank**   Project: **p3j1**

```
Microsoft Excel - salary.xls
File  Edit  View  Insert  Format  Tools  Data  Window  Help        Type a question for help
G4          fx
```

	A	B	C	D	E	F	G	H	I
1	Employee Salary Projections								
2								Proposed	
3	ID	Lname	Fname	Department	Code	Salary	Raise	Salary	
4	4723	Collins	Geraldine	MIS	1	67500			
5	4389	Thibado	Adair	MIS	2	72500			
6	3829	Stack	Paula	HR	3	68300			
7	5843	Pensak	Karl	ACCT	1	73400			
8	6239	Herring	Ginny	MKTG	2	73425			
9	5482	Gatti	Al	MGMT	3	64720			
10	4739	Bond	Edna	MGMT	2	64500			
11	5325	Jones	Linda	ACCT	1	67810			
12	5284	Webb	Anna	MIS	1	85720			
13	6342	Gregory	Countess	ACCT	3	81500			
14	4739	Sawyer	Gloria	MKTG	1	72400			
15	4738	Burchfield	Trey	MIS	2	74315			
16	5329	White	Doris	MKTG	3	73590			
17	4389	Sugimoto	Tamami	MIS	1	73600			
18	3419	Milsovic	Nikki	ACCT	2	82500			
19	6384	Fleming	Rose	MGMT	3	72300			
20	5374	Wiggins	Parnell	HR	2	54700			
21	4793	Blakney	Mableleen	ACCT	1	67800			
22	5839	Ferguson	Catherine	MIS	2	72450			
23	5311	Wood	Julie	MKTG	3	71500			
24									
25									
26						Minimum:			

```
Sheet1 / Sheet2 / Sheet3
Ready
```

Tony's Salary Workbook Recommendations

- Format the workbook so that it is more attractive—use fill color, font size adjustments, etc.
- The entries are too close together. Increase row heights to 20.25 (27 pixels).
- Insert a blank row between the column headings and the first data line. Add an appropriate fill color to the blank row.
- Spell out the names used for column headings instead of using abbreviations.
- Sort the values by name before providing a printed list to Brandon.
- After the largest and smallest values are determined for each column, place a cell border around the values.
- Columns containing values should be formatted appropriately.
- Column headings should be centered over the respective columns.
- Insert a blank row between the last employee name and the first function formula. Add an

Client: _____ First South Bank _____ Project: _____ p3j1 _____

Adjustments Requested by Brandon Dustin

1. Delete the row containing Doris White.
2. Insert a row that contains the following information: 2388, Teague, Ronnie, MIS, 2, $68,700.
3. Name the sheet tab Salary Template.
4. Adjust column widths to AutoFit so they precisely fit the widest value in the respective columns.
5. Rotate (align) the headings slightly for the two columns that were added to compute the Raise and Proposed Salary amounts.
6. Add border shading for the amounts that were computed based on the function formulas for determining the smallest, largest, total, and average amounts at the bottom of the list.
7. In addition to adding a comment for the cell containing the title, add a comment for cell G5 describing how the raise was determined (based on the IF logical function formula and value in the Code column). Comments should print at the end of the workbook.
8. Include the following hyperlink at the end of the workbook as a good source for salary information: *Occupational Outlook Handbook* at http://www.bls.gov/oco/ocoiab.htm.
9. Salary figures will be included in a Microsoft Word document, so copy the workbook information and then paste it into a Word document so the information is in two formats: Word and Excel.

Formulas Needed for Employee Salary Projections

Cell Address	Formula Needed
G5	**Raise:**
H5	**Proposed salary:**
F26	**Minimum value:**
F27	**Maximum value:**
F28	**Average:**
F29	**Total:**

Business
Technology
Consultants

• • • Job Planning Form • • •

Client: _____ Project: _____ Job: _____

1. What deliverables does the client expect for this job? (Examples include letter, printed report, slide presentation, database file, template, spreadsheet.)

2. Which additional resources, if any, do you need in finding information to complete the job? (Examples include Internet searches and documents on disk.)

3. What software do you need to complete this job?

4. What special software formatting features does the job call for?

STUDENT LOG

Name: _____ Date/Time Completed: _____

Document File Name(s): _____

Comments:

Client: _____First South Bank_____ Project: _____p4j1_____

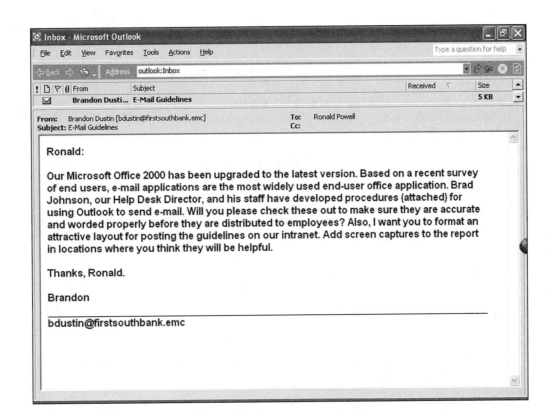

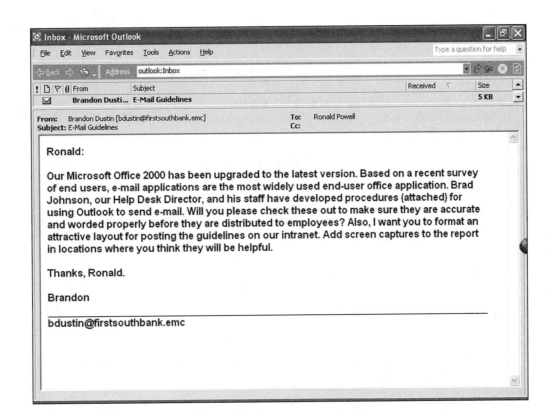

Job #1

NOTES

Files Needed
outlook.doc

In a follow-up phone conversation, Brandon Dustin requested that editing changes be tracked so that he can see what changes were made to the document. Procedures in the draft document relate to Outlook for Microsoft Office XP, but he asked that they be revised for application to a later version if one is available. Brandon also requested that BTC preview the final document as a Web page to make sure that its appearance will be attractive on FSB's intranet site for access by bank employees. (Ronald made a mental note to check with Tony Burdette for his recommendations.) Brandon stressed how important it is for all procedures to be formatted so that end users have a clear understanding about which parts of the text relate to instructions and which parts relate to a required keyboard entry. He also stressed the need for a spelling and grammar check. The draft Brandon sent begins on the following page. He dictated this additional text to add as a last item in the "Deleting Messages" section:

Tip for end users: Press the Shift key and then click the Delete key on the keyboard while pointing to an e-mail message to permanently delete the message without placing it in the Deleted Items folder.

Client: _____ First South Bank _____ Project: _____ p4j1 _____

Procedures for Effectively Using Outlook—Microsoft Office

These procedures were developed to help First South Bank employees use e-mail communications effectively. For additional information or suggestions, contact Mr. Brad Johnson, Help Desk Director.

Developing an Address Book

Outlook permits the user to store names and e-mail addresses in a facility called an Address Book. Procedures for making an Address Book are listed below.

Choose Tools/Options from the menu to access the Options dialog box.

Click the Mail Setup tab and then click the E-mail Accounts button to access the E-mail Accounts dialog box.

Click the Add a New Directory or Address Book radio button and then click Next to access a dialog box.

Click the Additional Address Books radio button and then click Next to access a dialog box that permits choosing an address book type.

Click Personal Address Book and then click Next to access a Personal Address Book.

Click in the Name text box and then enter an address book name, such as List of Clients (or another appropriate name).

Click the Path text box and enter the path where your address book will be stored. An alternative is to click the Browse button to locate the folder where the address book will be stored.

Click in the First Name or Last Name radio button under Show Names By Group to indicate how you want to display names in the address book.

Click OK. You will be alerted that you cannot use your address book until Outlook is restarted. Click OK two additional times to complete the process. You can then use the address book the next time that Outlook is restarted.

Adding Contacts to the Address Book

Client: _____ First South Bank _____ Project: _____ p4j1 _____

The address book can be used to store names and e-mail addresses. The following procedures can be used to store the information.

Assuming that you are in Outlook, click the Contacts button to access the Contacts view.

Click Tools/Address Book to access the Address Book Window.

Click File/New Entry (or File/New Contact) to access the New Entry dialog box.

Click the In The list box under the Put This Entry group and then choose the name that corresponds to your address book, such as List of Clients. Then click OK to accept the name and access the New Address Properties dialog box.

Enter the person's name and e-mail address in the appropriate text boxes. A short description can be added if desired. When finished, click OK to place the entry into the Address Book window.

Click File/Close or OK to exit the facility.

Creating an E-Mail Message

Outlook e-mail messages can be written while you are connected to the Internet or even when you are not connected. However, an Internet connection is necessary before the message can be sent to its destination. The following procedures can be followed to create e-mail messages.

Click View/Go To/Inbox to access the Inbox view. A shortcut is available to permit you to just click the Inbox icon to access the Inbox view.

Click Actions/New Mail Message menu options to access the Message dialog box. A shortcut is available to permit you to just click the New icon on the toolbar to access the Message dialog box.

Enter the e-mail address of the recipient in the To text box. (Note that you can click the To button to display a Select Names dialog box which permits selection of the recipient with a double-click if the name is in your address directory. In the E-Mail Type text box, enter this text: SMTP. Then click OK.)

The same procedure can be used to send an exact copy (called carbon copy or CC) of your message to another recipient.

Click in the Subject text box to enter the message topic.

Client: _____ First South Bank _____ Project: _____ p4j1 _____

Click in the text box to enter the text for the message that you want to send to the recipient.

Finally, click the Send button to transmit your message to the recipient. (Note: If the spell checking function is operative, Outlook will check for misspelled words before sending the message.)

Attaching Files

Files, which include Word documents, Excel workbooks, PowerPoint presentations, Access databases, photographs, diagrams, and many other types of files, can be attached to your e-mail message. The recipient can then view the file in its original form.

The first step is to create your e-mail message in the usual manner.

Click Insert/File from the menu to access the Insert File dialog box.

Locate the file that you want to attach and then click the name of the file. Then, click the Insert button. An icon will be displayed next to your message to indicate that a file is attached to your e-mail message.

Click the Send button to transmit your e-mail message and attachment.

Viewing E-Mail Messages

Reading messages with Outlook works well with most service providers, with the exception of America Online. The following procedures can be followed to view your e-mail messages.

Choose View/Go To/Inbox to access the Inbox view. A shortcut is available to permit you to click the Inbox icon while in Outlook to access the Inbox view.

Click Tools/Send/Receive to access a listing of Internet accounts that have been established.

Click the Internet account that corresponds to your account to access a list of messages that have been sent to you.

Double-click the name or subject of the e-mail message that you want to view. If an attachment is available with the message, you may need to click the icon to access the message and attachment. Then double-click the name of the file to access the attached document.

Click Close or File/Exit to exit the facility.

Business Technology Consultants
Project and Job Information

Client: **First South Bank**   Project: **p4j1**

Replying to or Forwarding Messages

While the e-mail message is open, click the Reply button on the toolbar. Enter the text for your reply and then click the Send button.

While the e-mail message is open, click the Forward button on the toolbar to access the Messages dialog box. Enter the e-mail address of the desired recipient and then click the Send button.

Deleting Messages

While viewing the list of e-mail messages, click the message that you desire to delete and then press the Delete button on the keyboard or click the Delete button on the toolbar.

The above procedure places the deleted messages into a Deleted Items folder. To permanently delete the messages, click the Deleted Items icon on the Outlook bar. Click the message or messages that you want to delete and then press the Delete key on the keyboard. Click the Yes button to confirm that you want to delete the messages.

Using Outlook Shortcuts

Outlook provides shortcuts that can be used to quickly access many commonly performed functions. Available shortcuts include Outlook Today, Inbox, Sent Items, Deleted Items, Calendar, Contacts, Tasks, and Notes. Check to see if these shortcuts are available with your configuration. If not, contact Help Desk personnel for assistance.

Client: _____ First South Bank _____ Project: _____ p4j1 _____

Recommendations from Tony Burdette

➢ Each group of instructions should be placed into a separate table with an appropriate fill and font color design layout to contrast with the document theme color and background.

➢ Employees will need to view dialog boxes to make sure they have accessed the appropriate screen in Outlook. Each dialog box screen (and other screens as appropriate) should be captured (copied) and then pasted to the document at the location where the dialog box is introduced.

➢ Number each set of instructional steps within each category to make it easier for FSB employees to follow instructions. This will also provide a good reference point if assistance from the help desk is needed.

➢ An endnote reference should be made that instructions are based on Microsoft Office Outlook. The notation should be made to the title with the referenced statement appearing at the end of the document.

➢ Format text with boldface or color to highlight instructions that require action from end users. An example for each procedure is shown below. Also, sectional headings should be placed in a table format with attractive fill and font colors.

Example 1: Highlighting Instructions
Enter the e-mail address of the recipient in the **To** text box. (Note that you can click the **To** button to display a **Select Names** dialog box which permits selection of the recipient with a double-click if the name is in your address directory. In the **E-Mail Type:** text box, enter this text: **SMTP**. Then click **OK**.)

Example 2: Highlighting Instructions
Click **Actions/New Mail Message** menu options to access the **Message** dialog box. A shortcut is available to permit you to just click the **New** icon on the toolbar to access the **Message** dialog box.

➢ For Web formatting, select a theme style from the following list: Clearday, Corporate, Blocks, Blends, or Automobile. A form for evaluating these styles is provided. Experiment with each theme and then choose the one that has the best appearance on the Web.

➢ Experiment with several styles from the Styles Gallery to determine the one that provides the best appearance. I hesitate to recommend a style until after you have completed the document and have had an opportunity to see how the style and theme can be coordinated for the most attractive overall format.

Business Technology Consultants
• Project and Job Information •

Client: _____ First South Bank _____ Project: _____ p4j1 _____

Theme	Theme Evaluation		
	Excellent	Good	Fair
Clearday			
Comments:			
Corporate			
Comments:			
Blocks			
Comments:			
Blends			
Comments:			
Automobile			
Comments:			

• • • Job Planning Form • • •

Client: _____ Project: _____ Job: _____

1. What deliverables does the client expect for this job? (Examples include letter, printed report, slide presentation, database file, template, spreadsheet.)

2. Which additional resources, if any, do you need in finding information to complete the job? (Examples include Internet searches and documents on disk.)

3. What software do you need to complete this job?

4. What special software formatting features does the job call for?

STUDENT LOG

Name: _____ Date/Time Completed: _____

Document File Name(s): _____

Comments:

Client: _____First South Bank_____ Project: _____p5j1_____

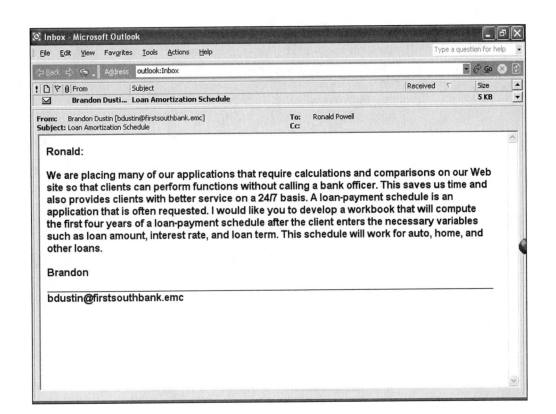

Files Needed
loan.xls

After sending the e-mail, Brandon Dustin called Ronald Powell to request that the loan payment schedule show a monthly computation that includes the loan balance at the beginning of the month, the interest amount charged for the month, and the loan balance at the end of the month after the monthly payment has been submitted. An amortization schedule that is available as a Microsoft Excel template is shown on the next page.

Client: _____ First South Bank _____ Project: _____ p5j1 _____

Job #1

(continued)
Files Needed
loan.xls

The workbook is protected except for the Enter Values section. Unprotect the workbook to perform any needed formatting changes. Format the workbook attractively for publishing on a Web site. Then protect the workbook again so that users cannot make entries with the exception of the Enter Values section. Brandon told Ronald he wants BTC to test the template with several sets of data that represent loans for home mortgages, automobiles, boats, and college tuition and expenses. He wants a printed copy using the values in the table shown on the next page.

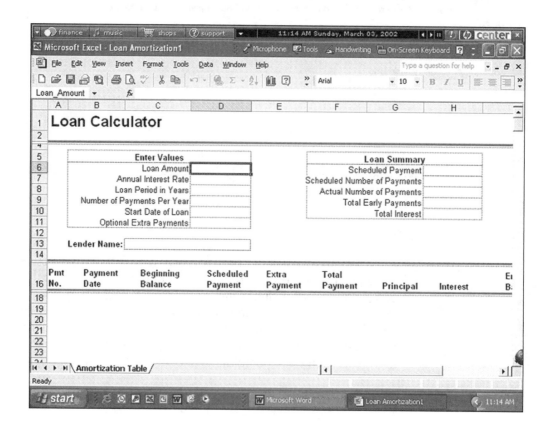

Client: _____ First South Bank _____ Project: _____ p5j1 _____

Entry Label	Value
Loan Amount	**$36,000**
Annual Interest Rate	**6.9%**
Loan Period in Years	**4**
Number of Payments Per Year	**12**
Start Date of Loan	Note: Enter the date for the first day of next month.
Lender Name	**Joy Kinard**

Job Planning Form

Client: _____ Project: _____ Job: _____

1. What deliverables does the client expect for this job? (Examples include letter, printed report, slide presentation, database file, template, spreadsheet.)

2. Which additional resources, if any, do you need in finding information to complete the job? (Examples include Internet searches and documents on disk.)

3. What software do you need to complete this job?

4. What special software formatting features does the job call for?

STUDENT LOG

Name: _____ Date/Time Completed: _____

Document File Name(s): _____

Comments:

Client: **First South Bank** Project: **p6j1**

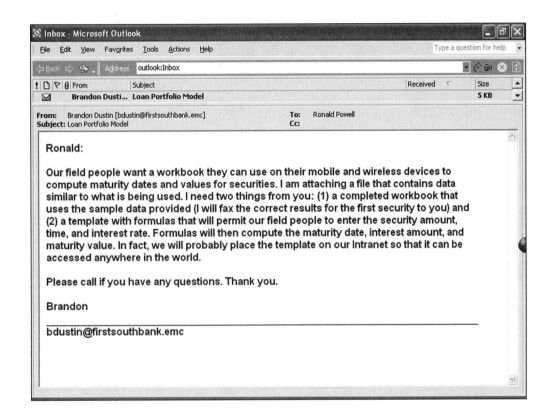

Job #1

Files Needed
portfolio.xls

The workbook Brandon Dustin attached is on the next page. When Ronald Powell called Brandon, Brandon told him to make sure that the interest rate formula uses a 360-day year to compute the interest amount and maturity value for each security. Tanya LeFebre, BTC's director of graphic design, advised Ronald that the following formula will compute the interest amount: security amount multiplied by the time divided by 360 multiplied by the interest rate. The original security amount added to the interest amount results in the maturity value. A meeting with Tanya and a subsequent conference call with Brandon indicated several additional considerations which are listed below the workbook.

Client: First South Bank   Project: p6j1

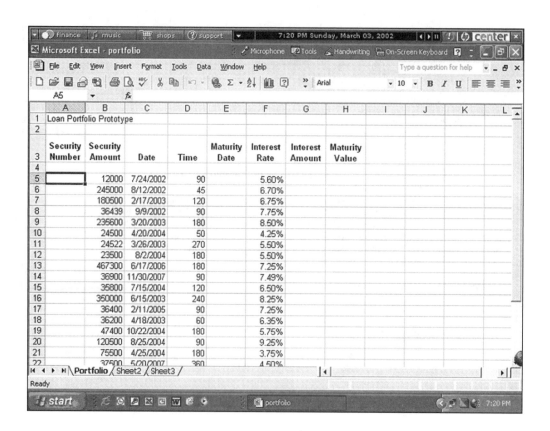

Design and Technical Considerations for Loan Portfolio Model Project (FSB)

- Data fill should be used to add consecutive numbers for the Security Number column to save keyboarding time.
- The Security Number, Maturity Date, Interest Amount, and Maturity Value columns should be formatted appropriately.
- The Freeze Panes feature should be activated so that the column headings remain on the screen as the end-user scrolls to the last row containing values.
- Formatting and Styles should be used to make the workbook attractive enough to go on the FSB Intranet.
- Protection should be activated for all cells where formulas are located on the template so that end-users cannot accidentally change formulas.
- Align the headings for the Date and Time columns so that each one slants upward at a 45-degree angle.

Client: **First South Bank** Project: **p6j1**

Job #1

(continued)
Files Needed
portfolio.xls

The values Brandon faxed will show if the formulas are working properly. Tanya gave Ronald two planning forms that will be useful for developing formulas and planning for cell protection. Copy the formulas to the remainder of the workbook columns. Formulas for cells G31 and H31 should compute the total interest and total maturity value amounts.

Brandon wants a printed copy of the completed workbook and of the template.

Sample Computed Values for the First Security

Security No.	Maturity Date	Interest Amount	Maturity Value
1	10/22/2002	$168.00	$12,168.00

Planning Form for Formulas

Cell Address	Formula
E5	
G5	
H5	
G31	
H31	

Planning Form for Protected Cells

Range Number	Cell Range to be Protected
One	
Two	
Three	
Four	

· · · Job Planning Form · · ·

Client: _____ Project: _____ Job: _____

1. What deliverables does the client expect for this job? (Examples include letter, printed report, slide presentation, database file, template, spreadsheet.)

2. Which additional resources, if any, do you need in finding information to complete the job? (Examples include Internet searches and documents on disk.)

3. What software do you need to complete this job?

4. What special software formatting features does the job call for?

STUDENT LOG

Name: _____ Date/Time Completed: _____

Document File Name(s): _____

Comments:

Business Technology Consultants
Project and Job Information

Client: _____First South Bank_____ Project: _____p7j1_____

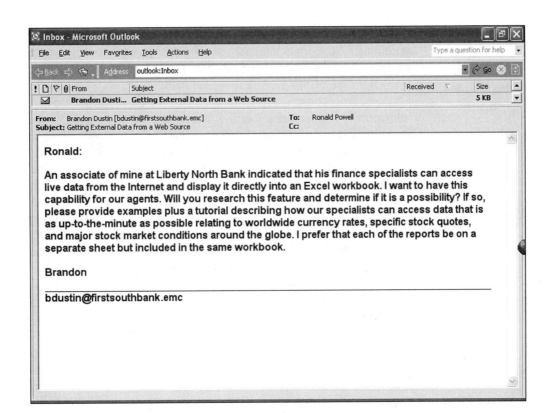

Job #1

Files Needed
financial.xls

The BTC research department told Ronald Powell that it is possible to obtain external data directly from a Web source in a fashion similar to the one Brandon Dustin wants to use for the FSB finance agents. The three sample sheets on the following pages indicate the types of data that are available through this process.

Sheet 1 shows currency exchange rates from major countries around the world when compared with the value of the dollar in the United States.

Sheet 2 shows data that were returned from a Web query in a near real-time mode, since the stock quotes are no more than 20 minutes old if accessed during a business day when stock markets are in session. Six stock listings are in the example. Brandon requested that quotations from ten companies of BTC's choosing be included in the example that is sent to FSB for review. Ronald's research team also told him that each company listed on one of the major markets (such as the Dow Jones Industrial Average Index) has a symbol that can be used to determine the information about the stock price during an

Client: **First South Bank**   Project: **p7j1**

Job #1

(continued)
Files Needed
financial.xls

Internet query. For example, using the AOL symbol will yield information relating to AOL Time Warner, Inc. Ronald knows he can use the Internet to determine the symbol for each of the ten companies he decides to include in the sample worksheet for FSB.

The research department indicated as well that stock financial information from markets in the United States of America (USA) is more beneficial when compared with relevant markets from other countries, such as markets in Japan and France. Sheet 3 provides a comparison of the performance of markets in the USA and other countries.

Brandon wants a tutorial with specific instructions that his finance specialists can follow to use Excel to locate financial information that is similar to what is shown in the three examples. He wants an appropriate name added for each worksheet that is developed for FSB. On the phone, he told Ronald that he prefers having the tutorial and examples included in a Word document with a printed copy for his review. He asked that the tutorial be divided into three sections with each section beginning on a new page. The content of each section should include the tutorial (with step-by-step instructions) followed by an example of a worksheet that will be provided if instructions are followed—similar to the examples provided on Sheets 1, 2, and 3. Of course, he wants the tutorial to be thoroughly tested to ensure accuracy and comprehensiveness.

Worldwide Currency Rates Compared to the US Dollar

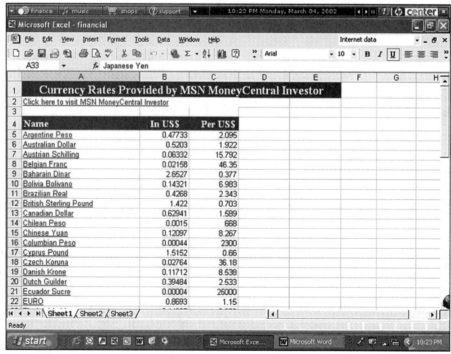

Client: **First South Bank**   Project: **p7j1**

Recent Stock Quotes for Specific Stocks

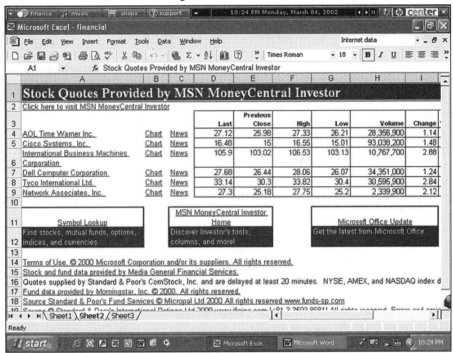

Stock Indices from Major Worldwide Markets

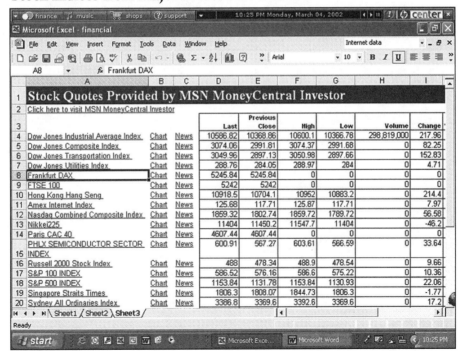

Business Technology Consultants

Client: _____ Project:_____ Job: _____

1. What deliverables does the client expect for this job? (Examples include letter, printed report, slide presentation, database file, template, spreadsheet.)

2. Which additional resources, if any, do you need in finding information to complete the job? (Examples include Internet searches and documents on disk.)

3. What software do you need to complete this job?

4. What special software formatting features does the job call for?

STUDENT LOG

Name: _____ Date/Time Completed: _____

Document File Name(s): _____

Comments:

Client: _____First South Bank_____   Project: _____p8j1_____

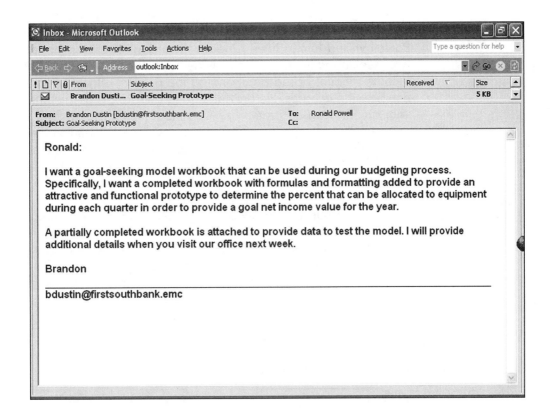

Client: **First South Bank** Project: **p8j1**

Job #1

Files Needed
goal_seeking.xls

Below is the workbook Brandon Dustin attached. When Ronald Powell visited him in New Orleans, Brandon requested that a goal-seeking value be set to provide a yearly $4,500,000 net income amount based on changing the percent allocation for equipment purchases. He provided notes on formula development with amounts based on the Expense Input multiplied by Total Revenue. He also provided forms for developing formulas for the workbook and for indicating values that should be entered in the Goal Seek dialog box to change the percent of revenue allocated to equipment in order to provide the established yearly income. These notes and forms follow the workbook.

Tony Burdette reviewed the project and recommended that column headings be formatted with the same fill and font colors that were used for the title. He also recommended that the fill color be extended across the worksheet in each row where it appears on column A. He cautioned that number formats and column widths should be adjusted as needed.

Brandon wants a copy of the completed workbook.

Partially Completed Goal-Seeking Workbook

	Quarter 1	Quarter 2	Quarter 3	Quarter 4	Total
Goal-Seeking Prototype					
Revenue					
Interest	$4,200,360.00	$3,760,400.00	$4,160,710.00	$4,900,720.00	
Services	870,900.00	654,200.00	830,720.00	810,483.00	
Total Revenue					
Expenses					
Administrative					
Marketing					
Support					
Bonus					
Equipment					
Total Expenses					
Net Income					
Expense Inputs					
Administrative	14.50%				
Marketing	15.75%				
Support	21.90%				
Bonus	375,000.00				
Equipment	24.50%				

Client: _____First South Bank_____ Project: _____p8j1_____

Formula Development Notes

- Formulas in cells B11 to B13 and cell B15 will be based on the corresponding percents shown in cells B20 to B22 and cell B24. Each of the four formulas should be entered with an absolute cell address for the percents to permit copying to adjacent cells.

- The formula in cell B14 should be conditional to provide a $375,000 bonus only if Total Revenue for the quarter is over $5 million. Otherwise, no bonus will be awarded.

- Appropriate formulas are needed to compute total amounts in cells B8 and B16.

- A formula to compute net income is needed in cell B17.

- Formulas should then be copied to compute values for the remaining three quarters.

- Appropriate formulas to compute total amounts for the year should be entered in column F.

- Appropriate column widths and value formatting should be provided.

Business Technology Consultants
Project and Job Information

Client: First South Bank Project: p8j1

Formula Development Planning Form	
Cell Address	**Formula**
B8	
B11	
B12	
B13	
B14	
B15	
B16	
B17	
F6	

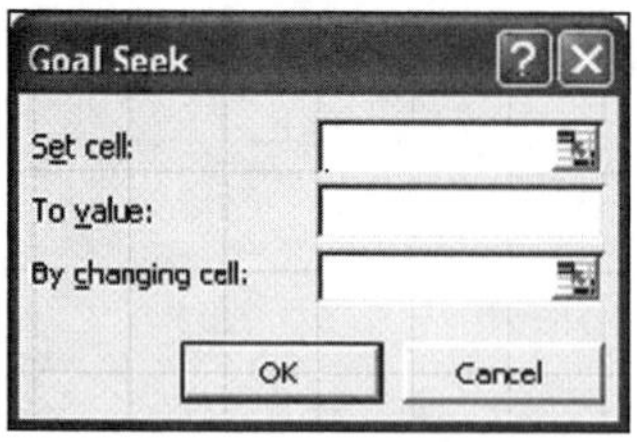

Goal Seek
Set cell:
To value:
By changing cell:
OK
Cancel

Business Technology Consultants

• • • Job Planning Form • • •

Client: _____ Project:_____ Job: _____

1. What deliverables does the client expect for this job? (Examples include letter, printed report, slide presentation, database file, template, spreadsheet.)

2. Which additional resources, if any, do you need in finding information to complete the job? (Examples include Internet searches and documents on disk.)

3. What software do you need to complete this job?

4. What special software formatting features does the job call for?

STUDENT LOG

Name: _____ Date/Time Completed: _____

Document File Name(s): _____

Comments:

Client: _____ First South Bank _____ Project: _____ p9j1 _____

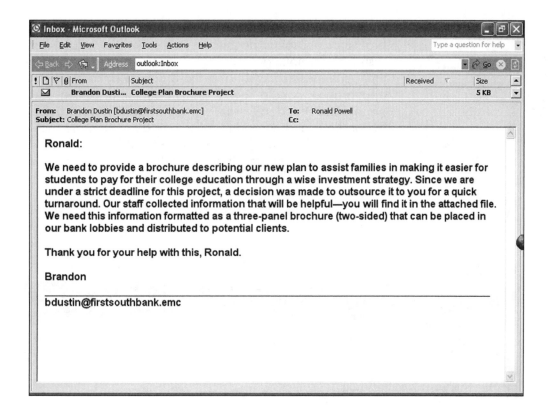

Client: _____ First South Bank _____ Project: _____ p9j1 _____

Job #1

Files Needed
brochure_template.doc
plan729.doc

Microsoft Word includes templates that can be used to create brochures and other documents, which will be helpful for this rush job. Formatting, inserting a clip art image, and providing other enhancements will give the brochure a more professional appearance. Ronald Powell printed out the document (see next page) from Brandon Dustin and reviewed it with Tony Burdette. Suggestions and comments from their discussion are included within caret brackets (< >). Brandon wants a final copy of the brochure. He requested that it be folded to show how it will actually look. Following the brochure text is a table for planning the basic brochure layout.

Partial Brochure Template

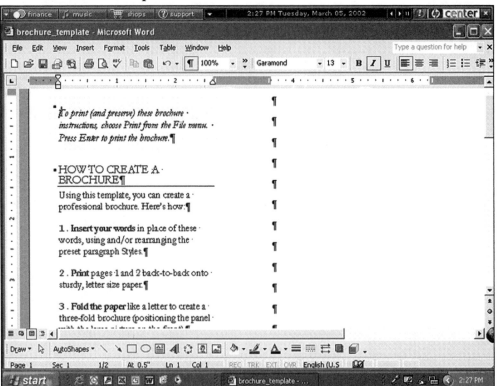

Client: _____ First South Bank _____ Project: _____ p9j1 _____

<FRONT PANEL FOR BROCHURE>

<Arrange the brochure title on the panel with an attractive font, design layout, and background. Consider using a watermark of a money-related clip art image.>
<Insert an appropriate clip art image to appear near the bottom of the panel.>
<WordArt can be used to give the title a more attractive design.>

There's a Better Way to Save for College—Plan 729

<TEXT FOR A SECOND PANEL>

<Locate and insert a clip art image depicting a family.>

College tuition is a large expenditure for most families. Predictions are that tuition expenses for a private four-year college will be nearly $300,000 by the year 2015. First South Bank has a plan to help you and your family develop a college savings plan to prepare for this big expense. Plan 729 will help you pay less in federal income taxes to make more money available for your savings plan.

College savings plan 729 was established under Section 529 of the Internal Revenue Code to provide future college students with a plan that provides for professionally managed savings options to meet college tuition and other higher education expenses. You may choose any accredited college or university to continue your education.

This brochure provides you with ideas about how you and your family can use First South Bank to help manage the investments for a higher earning potential.

<TEXT FOR A THIRD PANEL>

Potential benefits provided by the 729 plan

Ownership
You own your investment plan. An account can be established for your child, grandchild, spouse, another relative, yourself, or even someone else who may not be a relative.

Contributions
Several plans are available. Our professional staff will be happy to help you determine the one that best meets your needs. Contributions per beneficiary can be as little as $15 per month or as high as $10,000 per year up to $50,000 per child over a five-year period. Maximum contribution per account is $229,000.

Client: _____ First South Bank _____ Project: _____ p9j1 _____

Estate Tax Benefits
Investors can contribute up to $50,000 ($100,000 for married individuals filing jointly) per child in the first year of a five-year period without the requirement to pay a gift tax.

Income Tax Benefits
Distributions from 729 plans for qualified educational expenses are not subject to federal income tax. However, some state taxes may apply.

Flexibility
The plan is open to everyone. Fund distributions can be used to pay for qualified expenses (books, tuition, and room and board) at any accredited two-year or four-year college, university, or post-secondary vocational program in the United States.

<TEXT FOR A FOURTH PANEL>

<These items can be placed in a two-column table on the panel. Text that appears after the colon will be placed in the second column. A fill color will be helpful.>

Overview of Plan 729

Income limitations: None

Maximum annual contribution per beneficiary per year: $50,000 in the first year of a five-year period. No gift tax will be charged for this contribution level.

Taxation on earnings or withdrawals: No federal income tax will be assessed when used for qualified expenses.

Ability to change beneficiary: Yes

Control of withdrawals: Owner of the account

Investment options: FSB will provide several professionally managed portfolios.

Qualified use of proceeds: Any accredited post-secondary school in the U.S.

Penalties for nonqualified withdrawals: A 10% federal penalty will be charged.

<TEXT FOR A FIFTH PANEL>

Client: _____ First South Bank _____ Project: _____ p9j1 _____

Growth Potential Comparison—729 plan versus taxable accounts

The chart shown below provides examples to illustrate growth potential with $500-per-month contributions, an effective 8.30% return, and a 28% tax bracket. This example is shown for illustrative purposes only.

<This comparison can best be shown with a chart instead of text, as shown in the document.>

After 5 years: Taxable account = $33,429
                    729 college plan = $35,396

After 10 years: Taxable account = $70,301
                    729 college plan = $86,511

After 21 years: Taxable account = $153,703
                    729 college plan = $266,809

<TEXT FOR BACK PANEL>

<After folding, panel should be blank except for the following text—placed near the bottom of the panel.>
<WordArt will make the bank name more attractive.>
<A copyright symbol should be placed after the slogan.>

First South Bank
Building our business one customer at a time

Client: **First South Bank**   Project: **p9j1**

Form for Planning Brochure Layout

Panel 1	Panel 2	Panel 3

Panel 4	Panel 5	Panel 6

Business Technology Consultants

• • • **Job Planning Form** • • •

Client: _____ Project: _____ Job: _____

1. What deliverables does the client expect for this job? (Examples include letter, printed report, slide presentation, database file, template, spreadsheet.)

2. Which additional resources, if any, do you need in finding information to complete the job? (Examples include Internet searches and documents on disk.)

3. What software do you need to complete this job?

4. What special software formatting features does the job call for?

STUDENT LOG

Name: _____ Date/Time Completed: _____

Document File Name(s): _____

Comments:

Client: _____First South Bank_____ Project: _____p10j1_____

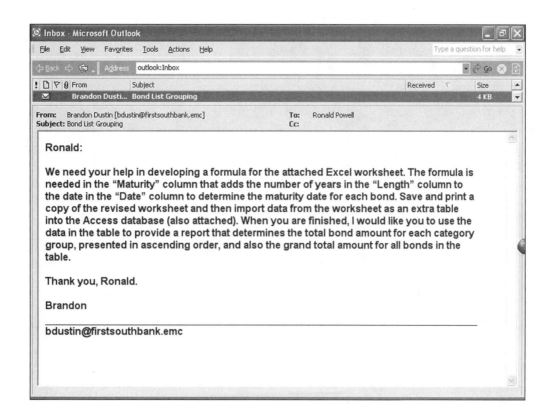

Job #1

Files Needed
bonds.xls
bonds.mdb

On the following page is a copy of the worksheet from Brandon Dustin. Ronald Powell's staff provided forms to use in developing the formula to be entered in cell E2 for computing the maturity date and in importing the data into the Access database.

Client: _____ First South Bank _____ Project: _____ p10j1 _____

	A	B	C	D	E	F	G	H	I	J	K
1	Bond_ID	Amount	Date	Length	Maturity	Category					
2	GT417	80,000	7/3/2002	30		AAA					
3	GT438	93,000	1/15/2003	20		AAA					
4	GT478	12,000	8/12/2002	15		AA					
5	GT481	85,000	5/24/2003	30		AA					
6	GT482	160,000	8/25/2002	30		AAA					
7	GT486	135,000	9/27/2005	20		AA					
8	GT492	171,500	4/29/2004	10		A					
9	GT497	125,400	8/15/2002	30		A					
10	GV117	135,000	8/1/2006	15		AA					
11	GV129	80,000	3/24/2003	25		AAA					
12	GV145	92,500	3/19/2004	30		A					
13	GV156	124,000	11/15/2002	20		AAA					
14	GV172	30,000	4/23/2006	10		B					
15	GV187	85,500	9/26/2002	30		AA					
16	GV192	22,500	5/16/2003	30		B					
17	GV207	80,000	7/12/2003	20		AAA					
18	GV217	90,600	9/30/2002	25		A					
19	GV223	20,000	5/23/2004	20		AA					
20	GV235	87,000	4/11/2003	18		B					
21	GV248	92,000	9/24/2002	25		AA					
22											
23											

Sample Bond Listing / Sheet2 / Sheet3 /

Formula Needed to Add Years to a Date	
Formula Needed in Cell E2	**Computed Maturity Date in Cell E2**

Steps Needed to Import Excel Data into an Access Database
1.
2.
3.
4.
5.
6.

Business Technology Consultants

• • • • **Job Planning Form** • • • •

Client: _____ Project: _____ Job: _____

1. What deliverables does the client expect for this job? (Examples include letter, printed report, slide presentation, database file, template, spreadsheet.)

2. Which additional resources, if any, do you need in finding information to complete the job? (Examples include Internet searches and documents on disk.)

3. What software do you need to complete this job?

4. What special software formatting features does the job call for?

STUDENT LOG

Name: _____ Date/Time Completed: _____

Document File Name(s): _____

Comments:

Client: **First South Bank**   Project: **p11j1**

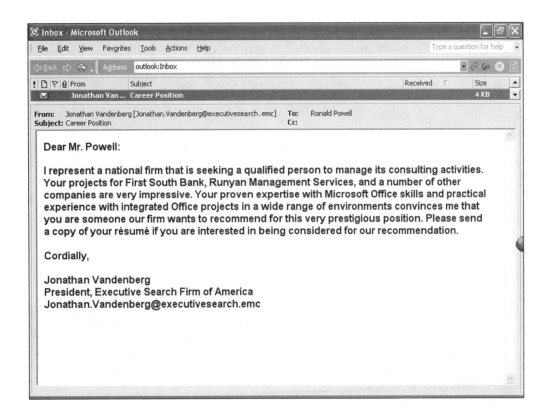

Client: _____ First South Bank _____ Project: _____ p11j1 _____

Job #1

Files Needed
None

Though Ronald Powell is not interested in pursuing a new work position, he keeps his résumé current in case an interesting opportunity arises. Microsoft® Office has two outstanding aids that help prepare résumés. One is a Professional Résumé template; the other is a Résumé Wizard like the one shown below. In addition, several résumé wizards are available on the Internet.

Use a Résumé Wizard to prepare a résumé that applies to your own educational training and work experience. Include a reference to your completion of integrated Office projects in a variety of workplace environments during this course of study. An envelope is also needed. Use an address of your choice.

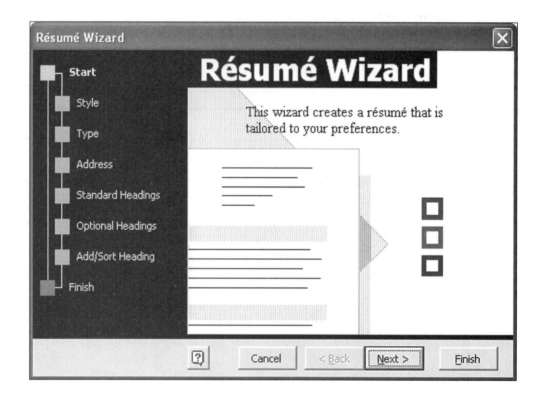

Job Planning Form

Client: _____ Project: _____ Job: _____

1. What deliverables does the client expect for this job? (Examples include letter, printed report, slide presentation, database file, template, spreadsheet.)

2. Which additional resources, if any, do you need in finding information to complete the job? (Examples include Internet searches and documents on disk.)

3. What software do you need to complete this job?

4. What special software formatting features does the job call for?

STUDENT LOG

Name: _____ Date/Time Completed: _____

Document File Name(s): _____

Comments: